Parita Shah
Priya Swaminarayan
Maitri Patel

Sentiment Analysis on Regional Texts Using Computational Linguistics

AF783785

Parita Shah
Priya Swaminarayan
Maitri Patel

Sentiment Analysis on Regional Texts Using Computational Linguistics

Looking into Lexicon-Based and Machine Learning Methods for Sentiment Categorization

LAP LAMBERT Academic Publishing

Imprint
Any brand names and product names mentioned in this book are subject to trademark, brand or patent protection and are trademarks or registered trademarks of their respective holders. The use of brand names, product names, common names, trade names, product descriptions etc. even without a particular marking in this work is in no way to be construed to mean that such names may be regarded as unrestricted in respect of trademark and brand protection legislation and could thus be used by anyone.

Cover image: www.ingimage.com

Publisher:
LAP LAMBERT Academic Publishing
is a trademark of
Dodo Books Indian Ocean Ltd. and OmniScriptum S.R.L publishing group

120 High Road, East Finchley, London, N2 9ED, United Kingdom
Str. Armeneasca 28/1, office 1, Chisinau MD-2012, Republic of Moldova, Europe
Managing Directors: Ieva Konstantinova, Victoria Ursu
info@omniscriptum.com

Printed at: see last page
ISBN: 978-620-8-43805-0

SENTIMENT ANALYSIS ON REGIONAL TEXTS USING COMPUTATIONAL LINGUISTICS

ABSTRACT

Social media is being used as a new source of knowledge by people of all ages. Using social media to express one's feelings in the form of thoughts and evaluations on anything and everything, from movies to businesses, products, and social events, has become a common practice. Analysis of the positive and negative features of an opinion or review is known as "Sentiment Analysis.", is a popular term in the industry. The systematic examination of online expressions is what is meant by sentiment analysis. Computer science, artificial intelligence, and linguistics all collide in processing of human language, or "understanding" by computers, is a long-term objective for a variety of human-like functions, including translation or question answering. This is a distinctive language processing (NLP) process for measuring the level of delight expressed in a written information collection or assessment mining. This strategy is used to determine what people think about products, services, and ideas. Emotional analysis of a film audit can decide whether a film survey is outstanding or pessimistic, and consequently the overall score for a film. As the machine generates and tests data, the most common way of assessing whether a survey is positive or negative may be automated. It has lately become a significant challenge to deconstruct the large amount of material available on the internet for Indian dialects to extract essential data. Because of the increased interest in Indian-language materials, it makes sense to take advantage of this sudden influx of information. Both Gujarati Lexicon sentiment analysis (GLSA) and Gujarati text machine learning sentiment analysis (GMLSA) are proposed in this study for the classification of opinions in Gujarati text cinema audits for opinion grouping. The accuracy of the machine learning and vocabulary-based techniques has been verified using five distinct datasets. A GujSentiWordNet opinion word reference is used in the vocabulary-based approach, and the opinion score is used to distinguish between feelings as a feature, whereas five classifiers are used in the machine learning approach: LR

(Logistic Regression), KNN (K Nearest Neighbour), RF (Random Forest), NB (Naive Bayes), and SVM (Support Vector Machines), along with TF-IDF (Term frequency-inverse document An evaluation model based on precision, accuracy, recall, and f-score is used to analyse the results of the analyses. When compared to the vocabulary-based technique, the machine learning-based procedure delivers more accurate outcomes, creating extra accuracy of 3 to 10% on average.

Table of contents

LIST OF ABBREVIATIONS

AI – Artificial intelligence

API- Application programming interface

BOW- Bag of words

CV- Count-vectorizer

CRF - Conditional random field

DT- Decision tree

FP- False positive

FN- False Negative

GLSA – Gujarati text lexicon-based sentiment analysis

GMLSA- Gujarati text machine learning based sentiment analysis

HTML- Hypertext mark-up language

HSWN- Hindi Sentiwordnet

ID3- Iterative Dichotomiser 3

IDF- Inverse document frequency

KNN- K-Nearest Neighbour

LR- Logistic regression

ME- Maximum entropy

ML- Machine learning

MNB- Multinomial Naive Bayes

NB- Naive Bayes

NLP – Natural language processing.

POS- Part of speech

REST- Representational state transfer

RF- Random Forest

SA – Sentiment analysis

SAIL- Sentiment analysis Indian language

SVM- Support vector machine

SVC- support vector classifier

TF- Term frequency

TP- True positive

TN- True negative

TOI- Times of India

URL- Uniform resource locator

XML- Extensible Mark-up Language

LIST OF TABLES

LIST OF FIGURES

1. INTRODUCTION.

People are always surrounded by internet-connected devices. Web access was formerly restricted to desktop and laptop computers, but mobile and tablet devices are now available, making it much more convenient than before. Aside from making our lives simpler and making business more efficient, technology has also enhanced our online experience. A place where individuals spend a lot of time, seek knowledge, discuss opinions, and even trade has emerged. What is the first step we take when making an online or physical purchase? To see if anyone else is talking about it, we go to a variety of websites and forums. Our first stop is to look at a few internet retailers that provide the items we need. We scoured the internet for reviews and comments regarding the product and the online retailer. It is only after reading several reviews that we determine whether to buy anything or not (1–7).

In the virtual world, most purchases are made after reading the opinions of prominent reviews and peers. Because of this, firms are now required to monitor and assess their online reputations. When it comes to a company's viewpoint, customer feedback and reviews are critical. As a result, no company can afford to ignore the value of comment and review analysis. It's called "sentiment data analysis" or "sentiment analysis" to figure out whether these are favourable or negative remarks, opinions, and evaluations (7–14).

Throughout history, the humankind has relied on the ability of language to communicate with one other. The sheer number of languages spoken throughout the world far exceeds our capacity to learn them all in a single lifetime. An individual raised in one area of the nation may find it difficult to speak with someone from a different section of the country. In today's borderless world, it's a problem we all must deal with. The English language is used to generate most breakthroughs and cutting-edge frameworks. More than a billion people inhabit the Indian subcontinent, which is home to a wide variety of languages, dialects, and writing styles. Without bringing NLP research and implementation in India up to level with those of languages like English, the vision of a Digital India for all cannot be fulfilled. Many people find it difficult to communicate effectively when using cell phones because of the language barrier (15–60).

It is possible to conceive a Google assistant-like smartphone app tailored to Indian people. If they could speak their native language, the system could comprehend their question and provide them with appropriate information from around the world. Because of this, there is an obvious need to support work on natural language processing (NLP) in Indian languages so that individuals who don't speak English may ask questions and receive responses in their own language (61–63).

The viewpoints of users differ from one another. As a result, it is necessary to consider a wide range of viewpoints to provide more realistic perspectives on the subject; thus, a big number of viewpoints must be considered. Most of the internet content is in English; but, as people become more aware of the media, information in regional languages is rapidly growing. Indian languages, particularly Gujarati, do not receive enough attention (64–70).

According to a literary survey, Lexicon-based and Machine Learning-based techniques (23,25,26,31–35,37–39,42,43,46–55,57–63,65,69,70) are used in emotion categorization methodology. ML computations are used to predict emotion in ML-based methods. The dictionary-based SA technique, on the other hand, employs opinion vocabularies. Vocabularies are delegated word reference based or corpus-based considering the assets needed to decide feeling extremity. The word reference method starts with seed feeling words and then adds equivalents and antonyms. The corpus-based approach, like the word reference-based procedure, begins with feeling seed words and then develops with a large corpus of evaluation words in a similar environment.

In this research sentiment analysis on movie reviews (reviews are created in Gujarati language) has been performed. Because Gujarati is a low-resource language, processing this type of regional language is difficult. The first task is to structure datasets because there is no informational record available that gives film reviews in Gujarati language; the second task is to pre-process data, for example, eliminating words, characters, or exceptional characters that have no significance; In order to better understand a particular text or entry, tokenization might break it down into a list of its individual terms, recognising features; and the third task is to generate feature vector using TF-IDF and BOW. The final section explains how the outcomes are formed after applying various AI-based and resource-based calculations to it.

Due to a lack of resources in Gujarati, the creators recommended and included dictionary-based and AI-based methodologies in their investigation. A dataset of Gujarati film surveys is created because there is no widely accessible dataset of Gujarati cinema surveys. The two proposed GLSA and GMLSA approaches are applied to a dataset of film surveys. It has been discovered that AI-based characterization produces more precise results than vocabulary-based categorization. The recommended AI-based process is evaluated using a similar method on five different datasets including a variety of actual data

2. LITERARURE REVIEW

The technique divides relevant work into two categories: ML-based and lexicon-based (71–85). Lexicon-based approaches need the development of a lexicon, which can be generated from an existing dictionary or derived opinion words from a corpus. Using the lexicon's polarity values, the general mood of the document is predicted. In ML-based systems, supervised approaches are often used. The progress of research in the field of SA for the Indian language motivated this review. Sentiment analysis is crucial for recognising users' perspectives, emotional states, and opinions, and sentiment analysis in Twitter is a hotly debated topic. Though various sentiment analysis studies in English have been undertaken utilising primary platforms such as government or news publications, there is a growing emphasis on social media content analysis to help in assessing community well-being or the perceived image of a product or organisation. This research highlighted and contrasted important issues in both Indian regional languages and English. It is possible to conclude that tweets in English are easier to analyse for sentiment than tweets in Indian Regional Languages. In the future, the research could be expanded by making and testing an algorithm that can analyse tweets in both Indian regional languages and English (86). For opinion analysis on Indian language, a dictionary-based technique and an AI approach were used as stated in table 2.1.

Table 2.1Opinion examination utilizing a dictionary and AI in the Indian language.

Reference	Language	Approach used	Dataset	Accuracy
(87)	Odia	NB, SVM, and LR- Ml algorithm used.	Odia Text	NB 81% SVM 60% LR 88%
(88)	Hindi	Lexicon based approach	Product review	Classifies review eithe in positive or negativ sentiment.
(89)	Urdu	Urdu setiwordnet (Lexico based)	Comments i Urdu on variou websites	66%
(90)	Malayalan	Malayalam sentimer lexicon (Lexicon based)	Malayalam text	87.5%
(91)	Hindi	Lexicon (HSWN)	4028 Hinc sentences (reviews o movies, products and trips writte by a wide rang of people)	59%

(92)	Hindi	Lexicon (HSWN)	100 movie reviews in Hindi text	Classifies review either in positive or negative sentiment.
(93)	English-Hindi	mixed word alignment approach for English-Hindi with Alignment Error Rate (AER)	270 English-Hindi sentences	64.59%
(94)	English-Hindi	Word alignment using a corpus-based approach	NA	Work as a better approach to creating an English-Hindi word alignment algorithm on a shoestring budget; word alignment is a common problem in the Indian language space.
(95)	English-Hindi	Naïve Bayes and particle swarm optimization		This improved approach allows users to select more appropriate Hindi queries rather than using a single translated query, improving overall performance.
(96)	English-Hindi	HindiSentiwordnet	Movie reviews	65.96%
(97)	Hindi	Lexicon- Sense-tagged Hindi corpus is created	Sense-tagged Hindi corpus	80%
(98)	Hindi	Hindi Sentiwordnet	Hindi syllabus	Classifies document either in positive or Negative.
(99)	Hindi	Naive Bayes (NB), Support Vector Machines (SVM), Logistic Regression, and Random Forest (RF) (LR)	General news headlines	RF- 75% SVM- 80% NB- 73% LR- 70%
(100)	Hindi Corpus prepration	Hindi wordnet	Hindi sentences	Hindi Wordnet was used to create the Hindi corpus.
(101)	Hindi	Lexicon	Movie reviews in Hindi	65%
(102)	Hindi	SentiWordNet lexical resource	Product reviews	61%
(103)	Taegu	Taegu sentiwordnet	2000 Taegu sentences	60%
(104)	Taegu	Telugu SentiWordNet	Telugu news sentences	74%
(105)	Gujarati	WordNet, Synset Replacement Algorithm (GujSentoWordNet), Bag-of-Words	Tweets	52.7%
(106)	Hindi, Tamil, Bengali	POS using SentiWordnet	SAIL2015	33.6%(Bengali), 39.28%(Tamil), 56.67%(Hindi)
(107)	English-Gujarati (Gujlish)	Deep neural network	Social medial blogs	Not specified
(108)	Malayalam	Malayalam WordNet	Movie Reviews	85%
(109)	Tamil	ME (Maximum entropy), KNN, SVM, DT (Decision Tree)	Movie Reviews	75.9%(SVM)

(110)	Hindi, Bengali	Sentiment lexicon	Indian tweets	43.20% (Beng: 49.68% (Hindi)
(111)	Hindi	NB	100 mc review documents Hindi	68.2%
(112)	Hindi, Marathi	NB,SVM	1200 Hindi 300 Mar sentences fi chats, YouT and twe comments	Hindi NB-61 % SVM-59 % Marathi NB- 57 % SVM- 61 %
(113)	Hindi	Hindi SentiWordNet	Movie review Hindi	Classifies revi either in positive Negative.
(114)	Hindi	Hindi Sentiwordnet	Hindi docum with 1000 wo	28.61 %
(115)	Gujarat	Support vector Machine	Normal total Tweets	92%
(116)	Hindi	Hindi Sentiwordnet	Hindi tw limited to character	Classifies tweets ei in positive or Negat
(117)	Bengali	Bengali Sentiwordnet	Bengali senter	Classifies sente either in positive Negative
(118)	Dogri	Dogri Wordnet using Hi Wordnet	Dorgi Lexicor	Dorgi worc prepared by link synonym with Hi synonym
(119)	Odia	Odia Wordnet using Hi Wordnet	Odia Lexicons	Odia wordnet prepa by linking synon with Hindi synonyn
(120)	Kannad	Iterative Dichotomiser (Decision Tree)	Movie review Kannada	79%
(121)	Urdu	Urdu Sentiment lexicon	Urdu sentence	Classifies sente either in positive Negative
(122)	Non English (compai ve study	Sentiment lexicon machine learning	NA	Both approach wc well but ML ba approach gives m accurate results.
(123)	Hindi	Hindi Sentiwordnet	900 mc reviews in Hir	80%

(124)	Malayalam	SentiMa- Sentiwordnet for Malayalam	Malayalam movie review	85%
(125)	Punjabi	Naïve Bayes and N-grams	News and blog dataset in Punjabi text	News- 74.1% Blog- 76.52%
(126)	Hindi	Decision tree	Indian Tweets	Classifies sentence either in positive or Negative
(127)	Hindi	SVM & DT	467 Hindi Tweets	SVM- 55.9% DT- 51.9 %
(128)	Malayalam	SVM, CRF (conditional random field)	Malayalam movie reviews	91%
(129)	Kannada	Kannada WordNet	General Document	Classified document into negative or positive sentiments
(130)	Bengali	KNN, SVM, DT, RF, NB	Bengali Horoscope	KNN- 95.9 % SVM- 98.7 % DT- 93% RF- 98.6 % NB- 93.08 %
(131)	Konkani	Konkani WordNet	Document in Konkani	Classified document into negative, positive or neutral sentiments
(132)	English-Bengali	Bengali sentiwordnet	Bengali sentences	66.54%
(133)	Gujarati	GujratiSentiWordnet	Movie reviews in Gujarati	62.62%

By far the most fundamental area of managing distinctive language is opinion analysis. It controls how information is presented so that the source of the content's inspiration may be determined. The cause can be due to good gratitude or research (negative). This study connects findings from several classifiers, such as multinomial naive Bayes and K-nearest neighbour. These strategies are used to complement or criticise a significant judgement. A complete cinema review datasets was made utilizing the acquired data and accessible proof. This study analyses how TF-IDF and word level Count-vector affect movie sentiment analysis.(134).

When focusing on Indian languages, sentiment detection is a fascinating but difficult issue. It becomes even more difficult when attempting analysing Gujarati language sentiment owing to the lack of enough resources. In this study, movie reviews written in Gujarati are subjected to a sentiment analysis model. The experiment, which used several datasets, demonstrated that it was possible to get findings that were improved by language. The Author performed preliminary processing on the data to get the desired results, which assisted in the generation of a set of tokens helpful in the feature selection procedure. The feature vector generated by the TF-IDF and Count Vectorise method is fed into a number of different machine learning-based classifiers, which subsequently generate confusion matrices to compare the accuracy of each classifier. This study also notes that the proposed model may have minor changes in accuracy when applied to various datasets, but overall, the results were encouraging. (135).

In this study, the authors put twelve methods for boosting classifier efficiency through their paces across three datasets with varying class distributions (50:50, 20:80, and 5:95). The researchers sought to evaluate the efficacy of ensemble learning, data sampling, and feature selection. Results from statistical testing showed that the balanced dataset and the 20:80 unbalanced dataset both benefited from the use of feature selection strategies (136). This research surveys the many methods of feature selection that have been offered. Several state-of-the-art methods for selecting features are introduced. It is clear from their testing that some sort of criteria must be established. However, in reality, we have no way of knowing which parameters are most suited for the available data. Future work will hopefully provide light on how to optimally pick the adaptive hyper-parameters and how many features to use in the final model (137). Success using language vector representations has been established in a number of NLP applications. This study's goal is to learn how well word vector representations function for the sentiment analysis challenge. Particular attention is paid to the three tasks of "extraction of sentiment words," "identification of polarity of sentiment words," and "prediction of emotion in text." They evaluate the quality of domain-dependent vectors and explore the effectiveness of vector representations over different text data sets. Many vector-based qualities have been computed using vector representations, and their effectiveness has been tested systematically. Using only simple vector-based features, they were able to do text sentiment analysis of APP evaluations with an F1 of 85.77%, a recall of 85.20%, and an accuracy of 86.35%. (138).

The vast amount of user-generated content needs reliable methods for analysing and defining ideas and perspectives. The authors of this study set out to learn how feature selection impacts the sentiment analysis of Greek online comments. Several text-based and part-of-speech-based features are provided, along with a basic approach for evaluating text and determining opinion. The results of the test show that the method works for recognising different points of view in Greek text and give insight into the factors that contribute to the accuracy of categorization (139).

These days, everyone has a means through which they may share their individuality with the world. In today's highly evolved and updated world, Facebook, WhatsApp, and Twitter are just a few examples of the many social media websites and Android apps that are inundated with users and information. There are few services as popular and utilised as Twitter. Comments on this are often seen as the major means of expressing one's emotions, and hence are favoured by virtually everyone who is enthusiastic or sociable. One might get a sense of the speakers' attitudes and emotions from their comments. Due to the unstructured nature of the material on these platforms, preparatory processing is required prior to any meaningful analysis. Features are obtained from the processed data, which is prepared using one of six methods. Feature extraction may be accomplished in a number of different ways; some examples are the Bag of Words approach, the TF-IDF method, word embedding, and NLP (natural language processing)-based features like word count and noun count. In this research, they looked at how the TF-IDF word level and N-Gram affected the sentiment analysis Tweet dataset. They discovered that TF-IDF (Term Frequency-Inverse Document Frequency) word level features outperform N-gram features in sentiment analysis by 3-4%. We consider six distinct classification strategies (SVM, DT, KNN, RF, LR, NB) and their corresponding performance metrics (Accuracy, F-score, Precision, and Recall) for this study. (140).

In the midst of the COVID-19 outbreak, the e-commerce site has amassed a large amount of up-to-the-minute information on product ratings and comments. Businesses can't effectively compete in today's market without rating and review systems that enable them to immediately expose consumers' true opinions of their products and services and use this information to inform and refine future offerings. Amazon is one website that may provide an abundance of data on customer reviews. Unfortunately, product review data is typically disorganised and difficult to handle. This experimental study analysed the effect of text pre-treatment on the performance of sentiment classifiers Decision Tree, Nave Bayes, and Support Vector Machine (SVM) on unstructured data derived from product reviews. The Naive Bayes classifier has the quickest runtime, but the SVM's 88.13% accuracy makes it the superior evaluation model. Moreover, the results of experiments using our feature extraction method, TF-IDF, suggest that this approach can significantly improve classification accuracy. So, our method shows that a good process for preparing the text is very important to the accuracy of the classifier's predictions when dealing with unstructured product review data (141).

There has been a boom in the study of "big data" and related technologies in recent years. Massive amounts of data, especially unstructured data, are created every minute and second, and this has piqued the curiosity of academics. Much research is being done on text analytics and text preparation. In this research, we compared the effectiveness of three different machine learning algorithms for sentiment analysis after being subjected to a variety of preprocessing techniques. We applied many methods of textual preparation and studied their impact on the accuracy with which we could classify sentiment using three popular machine learning classifiers: Naive Bayes (NB), maximum entropy (MaxE), and support vector machines (SVM). Accuracy was measured for all three machine learning algorithms before and after applying preprocessing steps. The results revealed that the accuracy of the NB method was much improved by employing the preprocessing phases. By utilising the preprocessing steps, the SVM algorithm's precision was somewhat raised. Fascinatingly, the MaxE algorithm did not improve accuracy over the baseline. After including the preprocessing phases in the NB approach, the actuary once again performed much better than all other machine learning algorithms in our comparison analysis, followed by MaxE and SVM. The effect of textual preprocessing on the performance of machine learning algorithms is well established in this research. Also, it is said that the accuracy of the NB method has gotten a lot better since text preparation steps were added to the process (142).

In order to accomplish the classification objective, text must first undergo some form of preprocessing, during which features can be extracted. Due to the fact that pre-processing steps might affect the accuracy of the classification, many tests are run on the final datasets. We conducted experiments using many preprocessing strategies on three distinct datasets of tweets, one with no specified domain and the other two with specific subjects, to evaluate the effectiveness of four popular classifiers. Test results indicate that careful feature selection and representation can improve the precision of sentiment analysis. Unigrams and 1-to-3-grams work better than other representations, and feature extraction improves classification accuracy more than using all generated features (143).

3. AIMS AND OBJECTIVES

The internet provides a review on movies. Before spending money to a service provider, customers always like to read evaluations. However, in today's fast-paced world, no one has time to go through all the reviews, in addition, each review may provide fresh movie information or a movie feature. As a result, there is a chance that an essential user review may be missed. Film audit opinion assessment is a little later, and film survey in Gujarati dialects is still a work in progress. For a long time, neither a Guajarati-language film review dataset nor an evaluation tool for identifying key emotions in a film based on an overview written in Guajarati has been available. Up to this moment, the most complex technique for distinguishing opinion in Indian language has been vocabulary-based and AI approach.

As a result, our primary goals are as follows:

1. Preparing a movie review dataset: Collecting movie reviews from different websites to create dataset of reviews in Gujarati language.

2. Improve efficiency: To improve efficiency of proposed algorithm Gujarati text pre-processing is done by creating pre-processing technique and stop word list.

3. Feeling examination: To decide the overall population's assessment of a specific film, a dictionary based, and AI based technique is utilized.

4. PROBLEM STATEMENT

Up until this point, morphological, and lexical assets have been produced for a portion of the Indian dialects that have been considered for SA (Hindi; Bengali; Tamil; Malayalam; Telugu), but Gujarati has not been considered to the same extent for the Natural Language Processing (NLP) job of SA. Indian languages for which it has already been generated must be thoroughly reviewed, and it may be useful for other Indian languages in the future.

It's still a new field of study, although sentiment analysis for film reviews has been around for some time. However, no dataset exists that incorporates film surveys distributed in Guajarati, and no examination has been directed to decide the close to regional tone of movies considering audits composed in the Gujarati language. To predict public opinion in India languages, the most popular method thus far has been an artificial intelligence (AI)-based vocabulary-based approach. There is no standard dataset for sentiment analysis of Gujarati text, so researcher must generate their own. Researcher needs to invest time, effort, and investigation on their part. Text processing is necessary for a more accurate outcome. With no good dataset for analysis, it was difficult to apply Lexicon and machine learning techniques, but researcher overcame these problems and produced satisfactory results by using TF-IDF as a feature selection technique.

5. METHODOLOGY

5.1 DATA EXTRACTION

Data extraction is a critical step in large data analysis. Beautiful Soup library is used to successfully collect data from various movie review website. It's an open-source library that's free to use. A single seed URL can be used to automatically obtain reviews. A seed URL is just a beginning URL that navigates across all other webpages. Details of review collection from different websites are specified in Table1:

Table 5.1Details of extracted reviews.

Sr.no.	Website URL	No. of reviews
01.	https://gujarati.webdunia.com/movie-review (source language of this website is Gujarati)	232
02.	https://www.bollywoodhungama.com (used Machine translation approach to Convert reviews from English to Gujarati)	592
03.	https://www.filmfare.com/reviews (used Machine translation approach to Convert reviews from English to Gujarati)	396
04.	https://timesofindia.indiatimes.com/entertainment/movie-reviews (used Machine translation approach to Convert reviews from English to Gujarati)	572
05.	Collected reviews manually from users in Gujarati language	293

Data is used to train machine learning algorithms. It's vital that you provide them the facts they need to address your problem. It doesn't matter what kind of data you have; you need to make sure it's in a suitable size, format, and even includes relevant features. Python's Beautiful Soup module makes it possible to scrape movie reviews and other information. To scrape from a URL, the following modules are necessary. For HTTP queries to a specific URL, the Requests library in Python is an essential component. REST APIs and Web Scraping both rely on requests, which must be mastered before moving on. When a URI is requested, a response is returned.

HTML5lib is a Python library for processing HTML in pure Python. The WHATWG HTML standard is used by all major web browsers, thus it's built to be compliant. Beautiful Soup, a Python web scraping framework, provides the bs4: Beautiful Soup object. Automated programmes are used to speed up the process of obtaining data from a website utilising web scraping. Find below given steps that are used by Authors to create dataset in Gujarati language of movie reviews.

5.1.1 Import the modules.

To extract reviews from different website by using libraries listed in figure 5.1.

```
In [1]:  from urllib.request import urlopen, Request
         from bs4 import BeautifulSoup
         import re
         import pickle
         number_of_pages = 16
         all_articles = []

In [2]:  import urllib.parse
```

Figure 5.1Libraries imported for movie review scraping

5.1.2 Assigning URL.

Assigning the URL and generating a soap object will allow you to access the webpage's HTML content as shown figure 5.2

```
In [3]: for i in range(1, number_of_pages+1):
            url = 'https://gujarati.webdunia.com/movie-review/' + str(i)
            req = Request(url, headers={'User-Agent': 'Mozilla/5.0'})
            html_doc = ''
            with urlopen(req) as response:
                for line in response:
                    line = line.decode('utf-8')
                    html_doc = html_doc + line.replace('\n','')
            soup = BeautifulSoup(html_doc, 'html.parser')
            base_url = 'https://gujarati.webdunia.com'
```

Figure 5.2 Constructed a soap object to access html pages.

5.1.3 Extract the movie's rating.

Extract the movie's rating and other relevant information from the database. We are utilising HTML tags like href, title, and others to retrieve data from the BeautifulSoup object as shown in figure 5.3

```
    for div in rest_articles_div:
        all_articles.append(base_url + div.find('a')['href'])
    print('For ' + url + ' ' + str(len(all_articles)))
```

Figure 5.3 Acquiring movie reviews and related data

5.1.4 Creating list for reviews.

As shown in figure 5.4, create an empty list and save the movie information in a dictionary before adding it to the list.

```
        soup = BeautifulSoup(html_doc, 'html.parser')
        main_div = soup.find('div',{'id':'ram'})
        divs = main_div.find_all('div', {'class':None, 'id':None})
        divs = divs + soup.find_all('font')
        if len(divs) == 0:
            divs = soup.find_all('div')
        rating = ''
        for div in divs:
            if 'google' in div.text or ('રેટિંગ' and '/5') in div.text:
                if ('રેટિંગ' and '/5') or ('રેટિંગ' and '/ 5') in div.text:
                    rating = div.text.strip(' \t\n\r').replace(u'\xa0', u' ').replace(u'\ufeff','')
                continue
            article = article + div.text.strip(' \t\n\r') + '\n'
        if rating is '':
            elems = soup(text=re.compile(r'રેટિંગ'))
            if len(elems):
                rating = elems[0]

article = article.strip(u'\u200b')
article = re.sub(r'^https?:\/\/.*[\r\n]*', '', article)
article = article.replace(u'\ufeff','')
article = article.replace(u'\xa0', u' ')
article = article.replace('  ', ' ');
article = article.replace(' , ', ', ');
articlesAndRating[c] = {
    'url': url,
    'article': article,
    'rating': rating
}
```

Figure 5.4Listing saving multiple movie reviews

5.1.5 Categorization of reviews with rating.

Now that the list is full of movies and their descriptions, we can go on to the next step. The final step is to provide the details of each film together with a star rating as shown in figure 5.5 and 5.6 .

```
In [51]: df.head()

Out[51]:
```

	url	article	rating
0	https://gujarati.webdunia.com/article/movie-re...	\n\n25 વર્ષ પહેલા રજુ થયેલ ફિલ્મ ધ લોયન કિંગ હ...	3.0
1	https://gujarati.webdunia.com/article/movie-re...	\nફિલ્મ - ભારત\nનિર્દેશક - અલી અબ્બાસ જફર\nનિર...	3.0
2	https://gujarati.webdunia.com/article/movie-re...	અવેન્જર્સ:એંડગેમ મૂવી \nકલાકાર - રોબર્ટ ડાઉની, ક...	4.0
3	https://gujarati.webdunia.com/article/movie-re...	\n\n'લુકા છુપી (Luka Chuppi)'ની સ્ટોરી મથુરાના...	3.0
4	https://gujarati.webdunia.com/article/movie-re...	\n\nટોટલ ધમાલની સ્ટોરી એક પ્રાણી સંગ્રહાલય ધરન...	2.5

```
In [52]: (df['rating'].astype(float)<=1.5).sum(), (df['rating'].astype(float)>=3).sum()

Out[52]: (35, 115)

In [53]:
         import collections
         c = collections.Counter(df['rating'])
```

Figure 5.5List of reviews with ratings

```
In [64]: df_final.to_csv('Gujarati_Classification_Data_nov.csv', index=False)

In [65]: df_final = pd.read_csv('Gujarati_Classification_Data_nov.csv')

In [66]: df_final.head()
Out[66]:
```

	text	experience
0	\n\n25 વર્ષ પહેલા રજુ થયેલ ફિલ્મ ધ લૉયન કિંગ હ...	positive
1	\nફિલ્મ - ભારત\nનિર્દેશક - અલી અબ્બાસ જફર\nનિર...	positive
2	અવેજર્સ:એંડગેમ મૂવી \nકલાકાર - રોબર્ટ ડાઉની, ક...	positive
3	\n\n'લુકા છુપી (Luka Chuppi)'ની સ્ટોરી મથુરાના...	positive

Figure 5.6 List of reviews with positive and negative ratings.

After collecting reviews from various websites, each review is processed and normalised, and each review is assigned a rating of 0 (Negative) or 1 (Positive) based on the rating given by users on that movie, i.e. if ratings are greater than 3, 1 is assigned, otherwise 0 is assigned, as shown in figure 5.7.

	text	experience
0	વાર્તા એક સમયે નાની વકીલ મીરા કપૂર પરિણીતી ચો...	1
1	જીવનની વિવિધ પસંદગીઓ ધરાવતા નિષ્ક્રિય પરિવારન...	1
2	બદનામ આઇએએસ અધિકારી ચંચલ ચૌહાણ માટે વાર્તા જી...	1
3	વાર્તાસોલસૌથી અણધારી જગ્યાએ જોવા મળે છે જે સા...	1
4	વાર્તા તેને કબૂતરનો અનાસતો કહે છે પરંતુ મધુ મ...	0
5	વાર્તા જ્યારે પીટીના એક યુવાન શિક્ષકને નવા કો...	1
6	વાર્તા વિવિધ પાત્રો સાથેની અનેક વાર્તાઓ એક સા...	1
7	લક્ષ્મી વાર્તા રશ્મિ કિયારા અડવાણી તેને સંબંધ...	1
8	કોઇ રોમેન્ટિક ભૂતકાળ સાથે લગ્ન કરવા માટે તલપા...	1
9	એક કમનસીબ રાત્રે સ્થાનિક કેબી બ્લેકી ઇશાન ખટ્...	0
10	દલિત પરિવારની વાર્તા આયં મણિ નવાઝુદ્દીન સિદ્...	0
11	વાર્તા કાજલ સ્વતંત્ર જીવન જીવવા ઇચ્છતી એક યુવ...	1

Figure 5.7 Movie review dataset in Gujarati language

5.2 DATA PRE-PROCESSING

Data preparation entails adequate data fragmentation and data cleansing. In this study, we will utilise NLP preparation techniques such as stop word removal, tokenization and so on. Data preparation will result in more robust data with reduced noise. Figure 5.8. Shows the how pre-processing has been performed on

Gujarati text. In pre-processing, stop words does not have any effects on opinion expressed, so it must be removed for the normalization. Delimiters are used to split textual material into sentences, which are then broken down into words, which are then broken down into words is called tokenization. Tokenization is also part of the text pre-processing (141–151).

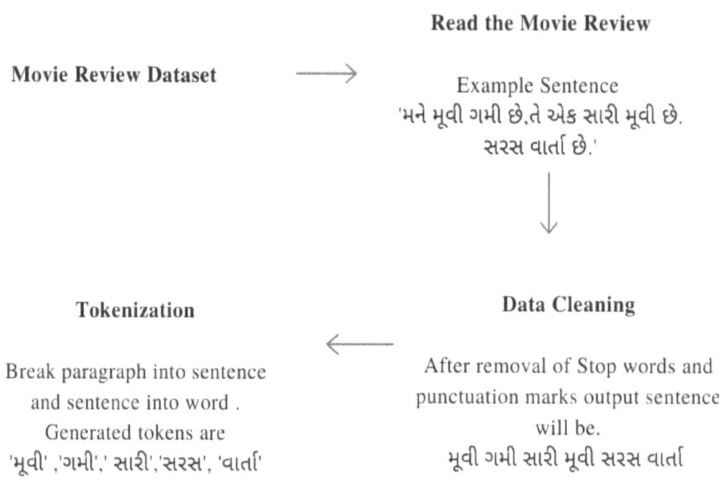

Figure 5.8 Gujarati text pre-processing steps.

When dealing with texts written in Gujarati, the following procedures are followed.

5.2.1 Import libraries for text pre-processing.

Figure 5.9 shows the required imported python libraries for Gujarati text pre-processing.

```
In [1]: import pandas as pd
        import numpy as np

        # text preprocessing
        from nltk import word_tokenize
        from nltk.stem import PorterStemmer
        from nltk.corpus import stopwords
        import re
```

Figure 5.9 Text pre-processing libraries

5.2.2 Load the dataset

Using panda's python library dataset loaded with reviews as shown in figure 5.10

```
In [2]: # reading csv file
        data = pd.read_csv("Gujarati_Classification_Data.csv")
        Sentiment_words=[]
```

Out[2]:

	text	experience
0	\n\n25 વર્ષ પહેલા રજુ થયેલ ફિલ્મ ધ લોયન કિંગ હ...	1
1	\nફિલ્મ - ભારત\nનિર્દેશક - અલી અબ્બાસ જફર\nનિર...	1
2	અવેજર્સ:એંડગેમ મૂવી \nકલાકાર - રોબર્ટ ડાઉની, ક...	1
3	\n\n'લુકા છુપી (Luka Chuppi)'ની સ્ટોરી મથુરાના...	1
4	\n\nટોટલ ધમાલની સ્ટોરી એક પ્રાણી સંગ્રહાલય ઘરન...	0

Figure 5.10 dataset loaded using pandas

5.2.3 Normalization and Pre-processing of Text.

One of the most crucial steps before diving into feature engineering and model construction is cleaning, preprocessing, and normalising the text. It makes it possible to standardise a document corpus, which is needed for the development of useful features. It also helps to cut down on noise caused by things like extra symbols and special characters, as well as XML and HTML parts. Figure 5.11 shows the required steps performed to clean the text.

```
In [5]: def clean_text(data):

            # remove hashtags and @usernames
            data = re.sub(r"(#[\d\w\.]+)", '', data)
            data = re.sub(r"(@[\d\w\.]+)", '', data)
            punctuations = '''!()-[]{};:'"\,<>./?@#$%^&*_~‘’'''

            # traverse the given string and if any punctuation
            # marks occur replace it with null
            for x in data:
                if x in punctuations:
                    data = data.replace(x, "")
            # tekenization using nltk
            data = word_tokenize(data)
            stop_words = ['પર', 'છે', 'કે', 'હોય', 'જ','આ','તેમ','માં','ઓ','એવા','નો','ની','આવે','એ','કે','જશે','થઈ','થાય','જ્યાં','કહે'
            data= [word for word in data if word not in stop_words]
            return data
```

Figure 5.11Method created for Gujarati text pre-processing.

5.3 TEXT CLASSIFICATION

Sentiment analysis is a popular topic of research in the fields of natural language processing and text analytics, and there are many resources available to learn more about it. Subjective content, in which people reveal their innermost ideas and emotions, appears to be the sweet spot for sentiment analysis. Sentiment analysis can be used in the real world to look at things like company surveys, customer feedback surveys, social media data, reviews of movies, places, and more.

Documents in the text corpus might range in length from a single sentence to many pages. Sentiment analysis goes under a few other names: opinion analysis and opinion mining. By combining methods from text analytics, natural language processing (NLP), machine learning (ML), and linguistics, unstructured text may be mined for useful insights. This allows for the derivation of both qualitative and quantitative results, such as the proportion of positive, neutral, or negative sentiment and the degree to which responses are subjective or objective. Sentiment polarity is often expressed as a numeric score that is derived from subjective variables like the usage of words and phrases that convey sentiments and emotions. A bad attitude usually has a polarisation of zero because it doesn't show any particular attitude, while a good attitude usually has a polarisation of more than zero.

Authors have attempted to get the general attitude from a vast collection of movie reviews. They have proposed two methods for sentiment classification on Gujarati text, one is lexicon-based sentiment classification and machine learning based sentiment classification.

5.3.1 Gujarati text lexicon-based sentiment analysis (GLSA)

In order to accurately categorise subjective terms like "sentiment," "mood," "polarity," "objectivity," and "subjectiveness," etc., unsupervised sentiment analysis models rely on knowledge bases, ontologies, databases, and lexicons. Lexicon models, also known as a dictionary model or a vocabulary of words model, are commonly used to analyse sentiment. These dictionaries often have words that show positive and negative emotions, polarity, parts of speech tags, subjectivity classifiers (strong, weak, neutral), mood, modalities, and so on. (23,25,26,31,32,34,35,38,39,42,43,88–91,133).

Using Gujarati SentiWordNet, an asset-based feeling examination approach aids in recognising opinions related to cinema audit in Gujarati language, where by and large survey extremity is assessed as excellent or negative. It's used to improve the precision of observing feeling synset substitution calculations, which helps in finding words that aren't in Gujarati SentiWordNet. The analyst has presented a dictionary-based technique for recognising the feelings of every film review available in Gujarati. To help us recognise sentiments, we created our own word reference called GujaratiSentiwordnet, which has roughly 3000 phrases, their linked equivalents, and the pessimistic and optimistic extremes of each word (71,78).

To assemble a word reference, Hindi SentiWordNet and IndoWordNet were employed by the analyzer. Hindi SentiWordNet is a commonly created opinion word reference resource in Hindi. Each Hindi SentiWordNet synset has three extremity scores, positive and negative, which are qualities that fall somewhere between 0 and 1, and the sum of these three characteristics is 1. IndoWordnet is a related Wordnet design that includes important Indian tongues from various Indian dialects. Python-based API IndoWordNet is now available. The question that synset can analyse dialects is the reason for GujSentiwordNet's creation. The term's extreme scores in Hindi SentiWordNet are likely to contribute to IndoWordNet synchronisation in this way. GujaratiSentiwordNet is being developed using word relations that are like IndoWordNet synsets (78,80)

The analyst has also used a machine interpretation method. Along similar lines, more Gujarati vocabulary can be covered, resulting in more exact results. It is deciphered using Google's understanding API for Gujarati translations. The extremity of these deciphered Gujarati words was determined using the Python TextBlob package.

Guajartisentiwordnet is depicted in Figure 5.12 with a list of words alongside extreme. The following are ventures for developing GujaratiSentiwordNet using Hindi SentiwordNet and IndoWordNet (133).

1. Using the IndoWordNet interface, map the Gujarati word w to the HindiWordNet synset.

2. Gather all the lemma synchronizations from GujaratiWordNet and use the IndoWordNet GUI to create a new lemma synchronisation outline.

3. The path to GujSentiWordNet development is envisioned using the synset extremity score (s-id) from Hindi SentiWordNet.

4. In Hindi SentiWordNet repeat process 1-3 for each word.

	POS_TAG	ID	POS	NEG \	LIST_OF_WORDS
0	a	10363	0.000	0.000	અનૌપચારિક
1	a	2627	0.000	0.750	મૃત,મૂએલું,મૃતક,મુડદું,શબ,વૈકુંઠવાસી,પરલોકવાસી...
2	a	11476	0.125	0.000	પરવર્તી
3	a	28106	0.250	0.375	સારી,સારું,અચ્છા,યોગ્ય,વાજબી,ઠીક
4	a	1156	0.875	0.000	ભાગ્યશાળી,નસીબદાર,સદ્ભાગી,સુભાગી,ખુશનસીબ,ખુશકિ...
5	a	2279	0.000	1.000	અભાગી,દુર્ભાગી,કમનસીબ,મનહૂસ,બદકિસ્મત,દુર્ભાગ્ય...
6	a	2384	0.000	0.875	બેઘર,આવાસહીન,ઘરવિહોણું,અનિકેત,નિવાસ_રહિત
7	a	4714	0.250	0.125	સુગંધિત,સુવાસિત,સુગંધીદાર,ખુશબોદાર,ખુશ્બૂદાર,સ...
8	a	1488	0.000	0.750	દુર્ગંધિત,દુર્ગંધવાળું,ગંધાતું

Figure 5.12 Reading text containing GujSentiWordNet

Figure 5.13 depicts the Gujarati word records generated by machine interpretation. The following are some ideas for making GujaratiWordList using machine interpretation (133).

1. Review the NLTK English Wordlist.

2. Read the Gujarati word w from the word list (which contains Gujarati word and its English significance)

3. Using TextBlob, extract a word's extremity and add it to the Gujarati word list.

4. Repeat steps 2 and 3 for each Gujarati word on the list.

	guj	English	polarity
0	મફત	Free	0.4
1	અખંડ	Unbroken	0.0
2	અખંડ	Akhand	0.0
3	અગ્રણી	Leading	0.0
4	આગળ	Forward	0.0
5	અચુક	Sure	0.5
6	ચોકસાઇ	Infallibility	0.0
7	સારું	good	0.7
8	દેવતા	Goodness	0.0
9	સારું	good	0.7

Figure 5.13 Gujarati words generated by machine interpretation

Figure 5.14. Demonstrates how lexicon-based sentiment analysis works in practise by allowing users to discern the tone of Gujarati-language movie reviews. (133).

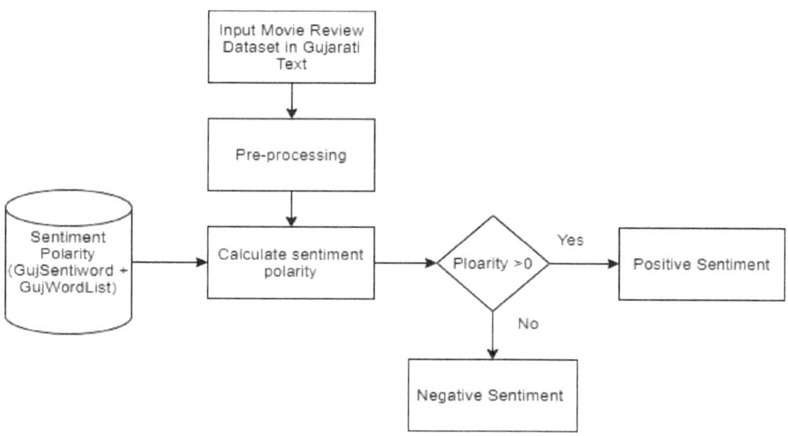

Figure 5.14 GLSA (lexicon) Based Film Review sentiment classification in the Gujarati Language.

In proposed lexicon-based sentiment classification method after performing text preprocessing sentiment will be calculated by mapping tokens to the GujSentiWordNet/GujWordList by performing steps (133) listed in figure 5.15.

The steps followed for identifying sentiment of movie using Gujaratisentiwordnet are given below:

```
For each review r_i in R:
  Apply preprocessing on r_i.
  Initialize variables pos_tag, pos, neg, pos_polarity, neg_polarity.
For each word w in r_i:
 if word exist in words_dict:
   pos_tag, pos, neg = words_dict[word]
     if pos > neg:
       pos_polarity += pos
     else if neg > pos:
       neg_polarity += neg
      else word in pos_data['guj']:
       polarity = pos_data[pos_data['guj'] ==[word]["polarity"]]
     End For
     if polarity >= 0:
       pos_polarity += polarity
     elseif polarity < 0:
       neg_polarity += polarity
     End For
```

Figure 5.15 Steps for lexicon-based sentiment classification on Gujarati text

To do lexicon-based sentiment analysis on reviews of Gujarati movies written by people, the following steps are taken.

5.3.1.1 Import required libraries

Libraries listed in figure 5.16 are used to perform resource-based sentiment analysis.

```
In [20]: # library imports
         import numpy as np
         import pandas as pd
         import seaborn as sns
         import matplotlib.pyplot as plt
         from sklearn.metrics import accuracy_score, f1_score, confusion_matrix,precision_score,recall_score
         from string import punctuation
         from nltk.probability import FreqDist
         from nltk import word_tokenize
         import warnings
         warnings.filterwarnings("ignore")
         # printing list of files available to us
         import os
```

Figure 5.16 Libraries imported to perform GLSA

5.3.1.2 Load GujSentiWordnet

Load a dictionary which contain a tuple for every word as shown in figure 5.17. Tuple contains a list of synonyms, POS tag, positive score and negative score for that word.

```
In [3]: data = pd.read_csv("gujSentiWordnet.txt", delimiter=' ')
        print(data.head(10))
        fields = ['POS_TAG', 'ID', 'POS', 'NEG', 'LIST_OF_WORDS']

        #Creating a dictionary which contain a tuple for every word. Tuple contains a list of synonyms,
        # positive score and negative score for that word.
        words_dict = {}
        for i in data.index:
            # print (data[fields[0]][i], data[fields[1]][i], data[fields[2]][i], data[fields[3]][i], data[fields[4]][i])

            words = data[fields[4]][i].split(',')
            for word in words:
                words_dict[word] = (data[fields[0]][i], data[fields[2]][i], data[fields[3]][i])

  POS_TAG     ID    POS    NEG  \
0       a  10363  0.000  0.000
1       a   2627  0.000  0.750
2       a  11476  0.125  0.000
3       a  28106  0.250  0.375
4       a   1156  0.875  0.000
5       a   2279  0.000  1.000
6       a   2384  0.000  0.875
7       a   4714  0.250  0.125
8       a   1488  0.000  0.750
9       a  29150  0.000  0.000

                                       LIST_OF_WORDS
0                                         અનૌપચારિક
1  મૃત,મૂએલું,મૃતક,મુડદું,શબ,વૈકુંઠવાસી,પરલોકવાસી...
2                                            પરવર્તી
3                  સારી,સારું,અચ્છા,યોગ્ય,વાજબી,ઠીક
4  ભાગ્યશાળી,નસીબદાર,સદ્ભાગી,સુભાગી,ખુશનસીબ,ખુશકિ...
5  અભાગી,દુર્ભાગી,કમનસીબ,મનહૂસ,બદકિસ્મત,દુર્ભાગ્ય...
```

Figure 5.17 Fetching GujaratiSentiwordnet for polarity calculation

5.3.1.3 Add new words with polarity.

A machine translation technique is being used to add new words with polarity as shown in figure 5.18.

```
In [4]: from textblob import TextBlob
        pos_data = pd.read_csv("guj word list.csv", header=None, names=["guj","English"])
        pos_list = pos_data['English'].tolist()
        pol_list=[]
        for i in pos_list:
            blob =TextBlob(i)
            pol_list.append(blob.sentiment.polarity)
        pos_data["polarity"] = pol_list
        pos_data.head(10)

Out[4]:
```

	guj	English	polarity
0	મફત	Free	0.4
1	અખંડ	Unbroken	0.0
2	અખંડ	Akhand	0.0
3	અગ્રણી	Leading	0.0
4	આગળ	Forward	0.0
5	અચૂક	Sure	0.5

Figure 5.18 More words are added with polarity for sentiment classification.

5.3.1.4 Clean dataset

Classification of text relies heavily on the process of text cleaning. Tokens are created by converting a paragraph into a sentence. During the editing process as shown in figure 5.19, all stop words, special characters, and punctuation are eliminated.

```
words = word_tokenize(text)
customStopWords = set(list(stopword) + list(punctuation+'|'+'||'))
wordsWOstopwords = [word for word in words if word not in customStopWords]
#removing numeric digits from list of words
wordsWOstopwords = [i for i in wordsWOstopwords if not i.isdigit()]
words = [i for i in words if i not in customStopWords]
```

Figure 5.19 Method for cleaning Gujarati text.

5.3.1.5 Sentiment Calculation

Figure 5.20 demonstrates how the negative and positive polarity ratings of the tokens/words in question may be subtracted to arrive at the overall sentiment of the phrase in GujaratiSentiwordnet.

```
#adverbs, nouns, adjective, verb are only used
allowed_words = ['a','v','r','n']
for word in words:
    if word in words_dict:
        #if word in dictionary, it picks up the positive and negative score of the word
        pos_tag, pos, neg = words_dict[word]
        if pos_tag in allowed_words:
            if pos > neg:
                pos_polarity += pos
            elif neg > pos:
                neg_polarity += neg
    elif word in pos_data['guj']:
        polarity = pos_data[pos_data['guj']== word]["polarity"]
        if polarity >= 0:
            pos_polarity += polarity
        elif polarity < 0:
            neg_polarity += polarity

#calculating the no. of positive and negative words in total in a review to give class labels
if pos_polarity > neg_polarity:
    return 1
else:
    return 0
#બધાય હો
Sentiment_score = sentiment("""એ કહેવું ખોટુ નથી કે કોમેડી ફિલ્મને રીતે બનાવવી કોઈ સરળ કામ નથી, અને તે સારી રીતે બની જાય છે,
તો તેની અસર લાંબા સમય સુધી છોડી જાય છે. 'બધાઈ હો' ફિલ્મ પણ કઈંક એવી જ ફિલ્મ છે. આ ફિલ્મ ક્યારે ખુબ મજાકિયા તો,
ક્યારેક થોડી બેવકૂફી ભરેલી લાગશે. પરંતુ પૂરો સમય તમારા ચહેરા પરથી હંસવાનું ગાયબ નહી થવા દે.જવાન બાળકનો બાપ જીતેન્દ્ર કોશિક ( ગજરાજ રાવ)ને
જ્યારે ખબર પડે છે કે, તેની પત્ની (નીના ગુપ્તા) પ્રેગનેન્ટ છે તો તે પરેશાન થઈ જાય છે. સોસાયટી-સમાજમાં પોતાની ઇમેજ પર ઉભા થનારા પ્રશ્નોના ડરથી તે
પત્નીને અબોર્શન કરાવવાની સલાહ આપે છે. પત્ની તેના માટે રાજી નથી થતી. તેનું કહેવું છે કે આ થોડુ પાપ છે. ત્યારબાદ બંને નિર્ણય લે છે કે તે આ બાળકને
દુનિયામાં લાવશે. ટૂંક સમયમાં મમ્મી-પપ્પાના આ નિર્ણયની પરિવારને ખબર પડી જાય છે. હવે ખબર પડે છે તો મોટો દીકરો નકુલ (આયુષ્યમાન ખુરાના) ઓફિસમાં
પોતાની ગર્લફ્રેન્ડ રીની (સાન્યા મલ્હોત્રા)ને ઇગ્નોર કરવા લાગે છે. તે શરમના કારણે પોતાના મિત્રો સાથે ફરવાનું બંધ કરી દે છે. તે સમજી નથી શકતો કે આ
સિચ્યુએશનને કેવી રીતે સંભાળવી. કઈંક આવી જ હાલત દાદી (સુરેખા સીકરી)ની પણ છે. દાદી આનો તમામ દોષ વહુ (નીની ગુપ્તા) પર લગાવી રહી છે.
તેમનું માનવું છે કે, આના પછળનું કારણ તેની વહુનું ટીપ-ટોપ રહેવાની આદત છે. પૂરા સીનમાં ઉથલ પાથલ ત્યારે થાય છે, જ્યારે આ સમાચાર સંબંધીઓ
સુધી પહોંચે છે.ફિલ્મના ડાયરેક્ટર અમિત શર્માએ પોતાના કલાકારોને સ્ક્રિપ્ટની સાથે કોઈ પણ ફેરબદલ કરવાની છૂટ આપી હતી. તેની અસર એવી રહી કે,
દાદીએ પણ જબરદસ્ત કોમેડી કરી છે. એ સીન જ્યાં તે કહે છે કે, 'સરકાર કી નોકરી કરે હૈ, સરકાર કી બાત હી ના સુની', 'હમ દો હમારે દો' કમાલ છે.
ગજરાજ રાવ અને નીના ગુપ્તા પૂરી ફિલ્મમાં છવાયેલા છે. જ્યારે દાદી 'આઈસિંગ ઓન ધ કેક' છે. નીના ગુપ્તાએ પોતાના અભિનયને પર્દા પર એવી રીતે ઉતાર્યો છે,
તેના પરથી લોકોની નજર જ ના હટે. આયુષ્યમાન ખુરાના એકવાર ફરી આયુષ્યમાન ખુરાનાના રોલમાં જ જોવા મળ્યો છે. આ વાતનો મતલબ તો તમે સમજી જ ગયા
હશો. તમને તેનામાં કોઇ ખાસ નવી વાત નહી જોવા મળે. તે એજ લાઇન પર ચાલી રહ્યો છે. તેમમે અભિનય મસ્ત કર્યો છે, પરંતુ કઈ એવું નથી કરી શક્યા કે
અન્યથી કઈંક અલગ તરી આવે. સાન્યા મલ્હોત્રાએ રીનિનો અભિનય મસ્ત રજૂ કર્યો છે. એક અલગ અંદાજમાં જોવા મળી રહેલી સાન્યાને પર્દા પર જોવામાં સારુ લાગે
છે. કુલમળીને બધાઈ હો એક સ્માર્ટ અને સારી રીતે વિચારીને બનાવવામાં આવેલી ફિલ્મ છે. કેટલીક જગ્યા પર ડ્રામા થોડો વધારે જોવા મળે છે, પરંતુ આ એક
એન્ટરટેનિંગ ફિલ્મ છે.""")

if Sentiment_score == 1:
    print("Movie is good")
else:
    print("Movie is not that good")

Movie is good
```

Figure 5.20 GLSA sentiment prediction output.

5.3.2 Gujarati text machine learning based sentiment analysis (GMLSA)

Figure 5.21 shows how an opinion examination model is applied to film surveys written in Gujarati. Trial and error on a few datasets uncovered that language-explicitly improved results were gotten. To achieve the ideal results, we did information pre-handling, which yielded a rundown of tokens helpful in the element choice errand. The element vector produced by the TF-IDF and CountVectorizer procedures is taken care of as a contribution to different AI-based classifiers, which create a disarray network against which the exactness of the various classifiers is tested. When the same model is used on different datasets, there may be small differences in accuracy, but the model gave good results (134,135)

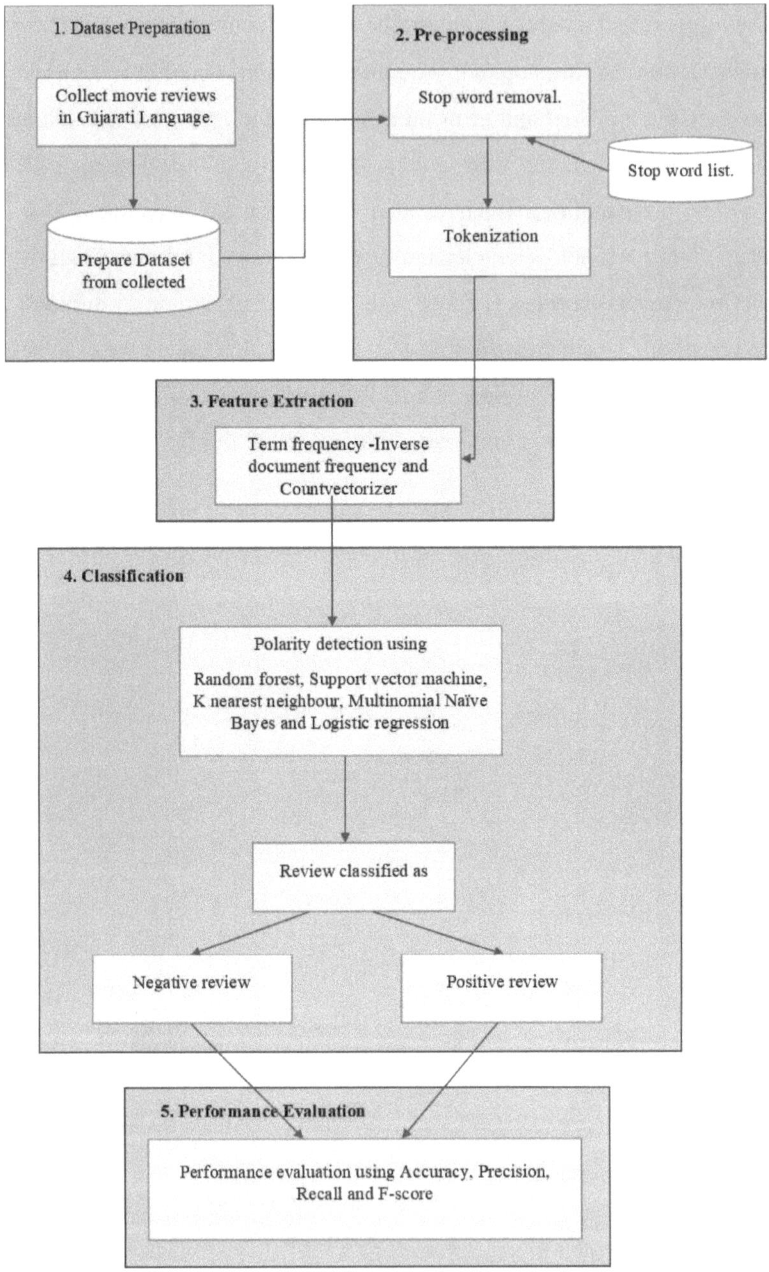

Figure 5.21 Machine learning based proposed architecture

To construct a model that understands and predicts the sentiment of text-based reviews, supervised Machine Learning can be used. To be more specific, classification models will be used to solve this problem. The CV and TF-IDF feature engineering techniques are employed in this approach. Following steps are incorporated to apply machine learning base approach on movie review dataset.

Following libraries are used to perform Machine learning based sentiment analysis.

5.3.2.1 Importing libraries

Figure 5.22 lists the python libraries used to perform the machine learning based sentiment analysis.

```
import pandas as pd
import numpy as np

# text preprocessing
from nltk import word_tokenize
from nltk.stem import PorterStemmer
from nltk.corpus import stopwords
import re

# plots and metrics
import matplotlib.pyplot as plt
import seaborn as sns
from sklearn import metrics
from sklearn.metrics import accuracy_score, f1_score, confusion_matrix

# feature extraction / vectorization
from sklearn.feature_extraction.text import CountVectorizer, TfidfVectorizer

from sklearn.metrics import accuracy_score, f1_score, confusion_matrix,precision_score,recall_score,classification_report
from sklearn.model_selection import train_test_split
# classifiers
from sklearn.naive_bayes import MultinomialNB
from sklearn.linear_model import LogisticRegression
from sklearn.ensemble import RandomForestClassifier
from sklearn.neighbors import KNeighborsClassifier
from sklearn.svm import LinearSVC
from sklearn.pipeline import Pipeline

# save and load a file
import pickle
```

Figure 5.22 Libraries required for GMLSA

5.3.2.2 Clean the dataset

Classification of text relies heavily on the process of text cleaning. Tokens are created by converting a paragraph into a sentence. During the editing process as shown in figure 5.23, all stop words, special characters, and punctuation are eliminated.

```
In [48]: def clean_text(data):

             # remove hashtags and @usernames
             data = re.sub(r"(#[\d\w\.]+)", '', data)
             data = re.sub(r"(@[\d\w\.]+)", '', data)
             punctuations = '''!()-[]{};:'"\,<>./?@#$%^&*_~‘’'''

             # traverse the given string and if any punctuation
             # marks occur replace it with null
             for x in data:
                 if x in punctuations:
                     data = data.replace(x, "")
             # tekenization using nltk
             data = word_tokenize(data)
             stop_words = ['પર', 'છે', 'કે', 'હોય', 'જ','આ','તેમ','માં','ઓ','એવા','નો','ની','આવે','એ','કે','જશે','થઈ','થાય','જ્યાં','કહે','
             data= [word for word in data if word not in stop_words]
             return data
```

Figure 5.23 Cleaning (pre-processing) the movie reviews

5.3.2.3 Transforming words to vector

For the purposes of natural language processing, vectorization refers to the conversion of a token into a numeric array that uniquely identifies the many attributes of a token. Vectors are used in the background to find similar words, group text into categories, and do other NLP tasks. Dense arrays have specified values for each of the array's spaces, and this specific array is one of such types. Instead of using sparse arrays with mostly empty spaces, prior approaches employed dense arrays (150-154).

Natural Language Processing relies heavily on feature engineering. Because algorithms and machines cannot read letters, words, or phrases, we must encode these words into some precise numerical form to interface with algorithms or machines. We are unable to provide text data comprising words, phrases, or characters to a machine learning model.There are several methods for extracting features. Some of the most common and extensively employed are: vectorizer of the count (Bag of Words model) and TF-IDF (134,135).

a. Vectorizer of counts (Bag of Words (BOW) model)

It's the most basic concept; imagine a phrase as a bag of words. The concept is to collect all the text data and count the number of occurrences. Then graph the frequency of the terms This technique is unconcerned about the sequence of the words, but it is concerned with the number of times a word appears, and the default bag of words model treats all words equally. sklearn offers all the essential feature extraction methods with simple implementation. For the Bag of Words model, CountVectorizer library imported and used as shown in figure 5.24.

```
In [ ]: # feature extraction / vectorization
        from sklearn.feature_extraction.text import CountVectorizer

In [36]: sentences = ['મને મૂવી ગમી છે.',
                      'તે એક સારી મૂવી છે.' ,
                      'સરસ વાર્તા છે.',
                      'દુર્ભાગ્યે કંટાળાજનક અંત.',
                      'કંટાળાજનક મૂવી છે.'  ]

In [37]: vectorizer = CountVectorizer(tokenizer=clean_text,max_features=5000, encoding='ISCII')

         # Generate matrix of word vectors
         bow_matrix = vectorizer.fit_transform(sentences)

         # Convert bow_matrix into a DataFrame
         bow_df = pd.DataFrame(bow_matrix.toarray())

         # Map the column names to vocabulary
         bow_df.columns = vectorizer.get_feature_names()

         # Print bow_df
         bow_df

Out[37]:
```

	અંત	કંટાળાજનક	ગમી	દુર્ભાગ્યે	મૂવી	વાર્તા	સરસ	સારી
0	0	0	1	0	1	0	0	0
1	0	0	0	0	1	0	0	1
2	0	0	0	0	0	1	1	0
3	1	1	0	1	0	0	0	0
4	0	1	0	0	1	0	0	0

Figure 5.24 Transforming word to vector by importing CountVectorizer

Data is first mapped to countVectorizer, and then features are created using fit transform().The function get features name() produces a list of all the words that describe a feature. Once countVectorizer is applied, the Bag of words will not be updated.

b. TF-IDF

TF-IDF is to normalise words in a collection of documents to represent how important each word is in relation to its document or phrase.

Term Frequency -The frequency with which a term appears in a document is referred to as its term frequency (TF).

A word's frequency is a measure of how often it appears in a specific phrase, or how common it is.

Inverse Document Frequency- IDF is a measure of the frequency of a term in a document. It's not important for the categorization if a term appears in nearly every document.

A word's IDF is equal to log(N/n) Where N is the total number of files and n is the count of documents with a term in them (word).

An evaluation of how important a word is to its sentence in a collection of sentences or documents is done using TF-IDF. For the TF-IDF model, TfidfVectorizer library imported and used as shown in figure 5.25.

```
In [39]: # feature extraction / vectorization
         from sklearn.feature_extraction.text import TfidfVectorizer
         vectorizer = TfidfVectorizer(tokenizer=clean_text,max_features=5000, encoding='ISCII')

         # Generate matrix of word vectors
         bow_matrix = vectorizer.fit_transform(sentences)

         # Convert bow_matrix into a DataFrame
         bow_df = pd.DataFrame(bow_matrix.toarray())

         # Map the column names to vocabulary
         bow_df.columns = vectorizer.get_feature_names()

         # Print bow_df
         bow_df
Out[39]:
```

	અંત	કંટાળાજનક	ગમી	દુર્ભાગ્યે	મૂવી	વાર્તા	સરસ	સારી
0	0.000000	0.000000	0.830881	0.000000	0.556451	0.000000	0.000000	0.000000
1	0.000000	0.000000	0.000000	0.000000	0.556451	0.000000	0.000000	0.830881
2	0.000000	0.000000	0.000000	0.000000	0.000000	0.707107	0.707107	0.000000
3	0.614189	0.495524	0.000000	0.614189	0.000000	0.000000	0.000000	0.000000
4	0.000000	0.769447	0.000000	0.000000	0.638711	0.000000	0.000000	0.000000

Figure 5.25 Transforming word to vector by importing TF-IDF vectorizer

5.3.2.4 Prepare your classifier for use.

You may use it for any type of text classification task if you supply it with the training data and labels as shown inn figure 5.26, which is what we're doing here for sentiment analysis (134,135).

```
In [6]:
    X_train, X_test, y_train, y_test = train_test_split(X_train, y_train, test_size=0.3)
```

Figure 5.26 Split the dataset for training and testing

Feeling evaluation is an AI tool that scans texts for the most extreme position, ranging from optimistic to pessimistic. Machines sort out some techniques to perceive assessment without human data by planning AI devices with occasions of sentiments in messages. To put it simply, artificial consciousness allows calculations to learn new tasks without being explicitly programmed to accomplish them. Assessment examination models can be prepared to look beyond simple definitions to comprehend elements like situations, humour, and turned words. To acquire good results, creators used LR, K closest neighbour, SVM, multinomial gullible bayes, and RF calculations to produce cinema audit datasets (53,66,67,87,88).

a. Multinomial Naive Bayes

The Naïve Bayesian Classification Method is a gathering of probabilistic calculations that depend on Bayes' hypothesis and the "naive" assumption that each collection of features is conditionally independent.

It calculates the probability P(c|f), where c is the class of possible outcomes and f denotes the provided case to be recognised, which represents some special qualities.

$$(class|feature) = P(feature|class) * \frac{P(class)}{P(feature)}$$

(1) Natural language processing (NLP) challenges are where Naive Bayes are most applied. The tag of a text is predicted using naive Bayes. They calculate the likelihood of each tag for a given text and output the tag with the highest probability.

b. Random Forest (RF)

The Random Forest classifier generates dozens of new suitable trees from a carelessly chosen chunk of the preparation data. As shown in figure 5.27, it is made up of a slew of choice trees (DT) formed from an arbitrarily picked subset of the preparation set, which then totals votes from numerous choice trees to provide the final forecast.

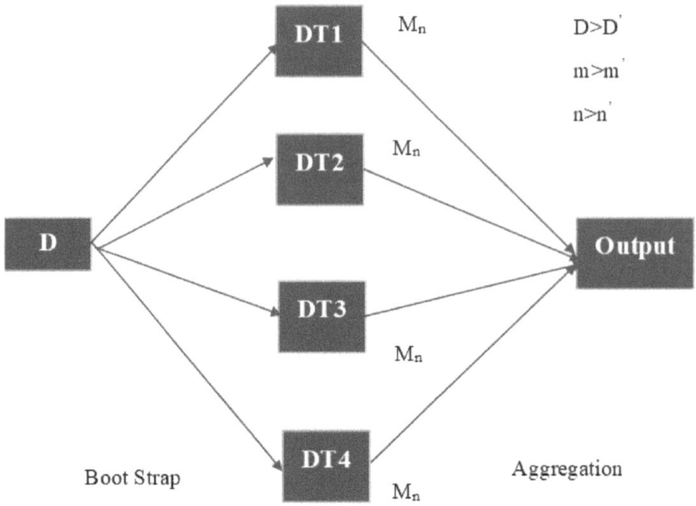

Figure 5.27 Model visualisation for the random forest

Every option tree has a large diversity, but when we combine them, the overall difference is modest since each choice tree is meticulously constructed on that example information, therefore the end result depends on multiple choice trees rather than one. The majority of the time, a voting classifier is used to determine the outcome of a grouping task.

A Random Forest is a programming methodology that addresses relapse and order difficulties by combining many decision trees as well as a procedure known as Bootstrap and Aggregation, sometimes known as packing in some circumstances. Rather than relying on individual decision trees to determine the outcome, the basic idea is to total a few option trees.

Irregular Forest employs a variety of selected trees as a central learning viewpoint. Column and element testing on the dataset is done haphazardly, resulting in example datasets for each model. This section is known as Bootstrap.

c. Logistic regression (LR)

To estimate the probability of an objective variable, the regulated learning order technique calculated relapse is applied as shown in figure 5.28. There are just two arrangements because the idea of the point or ward variable is dichotomous. In its most essential structure, the reliant variable is paired, with information addressed as 1 (meaning achievement/yes) or 0 (addressing disappointment/no).

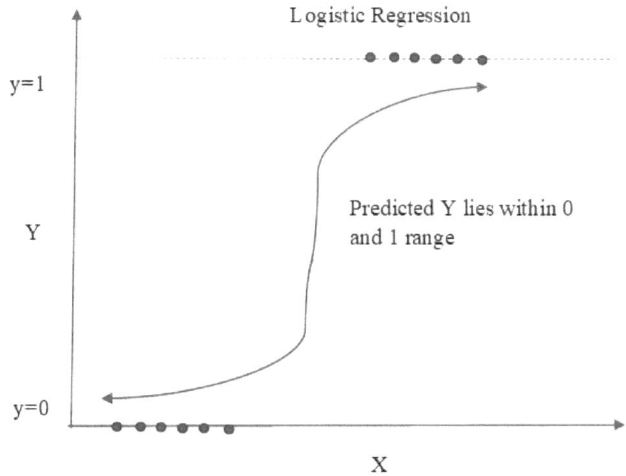

Figure 5.28 Model visualisation for the logistic regression

A strategic relapse model numerically predicts P(Y=1) as a component of X. It is one of the most key AI calculations that might be utilized to handle a wide scope of grouping issues like spam ID, diabetes forecast, malignant growth determination, etc.

The most fundamental rendition of calculated relapse is parallel or binomial strategic relapse, in which the goal or ward variable must be one of two sorts: 1 or 0. It empowers us to characterize the connection between a paired/binomial objective variable and numerous indicator factors.

d. Support Vector (SVM)

As represented in figure 5.29, a SVM model in multi-layered space is basically a portrayal of discrete classes in a hyperplane. To limit mistake, SVM will make the hyperplane iteratively. The objective of SVM is to partition datasets into classes with the goal that a greatest minor hyperplane can be found (MMH).

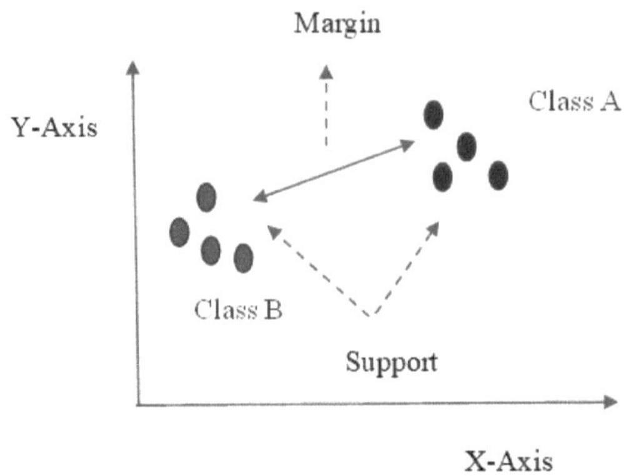

Figure 5.29 Model visualisation for the SVM

The accompanying standards are basic in SVM.

1. Support vectors are datapoints that are closest to the hyperplane. These information focuses will be used to draw an isolating line.

2. A hyperplane is a choice plane or space that is split between a bunch of objects of various classes, as found in the outline above.

3. The edge is the hole between two lines on the closest pieces of information of various classes. Processing the opposite distance between the line and the help vectors is conceivable. A significant space is viewed as a decent edge, while a little edge is viewed as a terrible edge.

The key objective of SVM is to segment datasets into classes to find the most extreme negligible hyperplane (MMH), which should be possible in two stages:

To begin with, SVM will create hyperplanes that best isolated the classes iteratively.

The hyperplane that appropriately partitions the classes will then, at that point, be picked.

e. KNeighborsClassifier

This methodology as shown in figure 5.30, is used to overcome the grouping model problems. The K-closest neighbour, or K-NN, approach provides a fancy line to organise information. When additional information points are obtained, the calculation will attempt to anticipate them as closely as possible to the limit line.

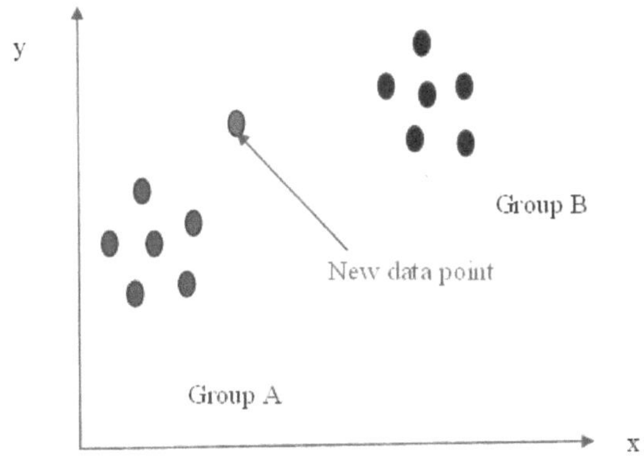

Figure 5.30 Model visualisation for the KNN

As a result, a larger k value shows smoother detachment bends, resulting in fewer challenging models. More modest k values, on the other hand, tend to overfit the data, resulting in confusing models.

$$d(x, y) = \sqrt{\sum_{i=1}^{k} (xi - yi)^2}$$

(2)

5.3.2.5 Defining and Teaching Models

Using scikit-learn library five different classification models (NB, LR, SVM, RF and KNN) are created and training data are supplied to perform prediction as shown in figure 5.31 and 5.32.

```
In [ ]: nb,rf,lr,svc,knn = MultinomialNB(),RandomForestClassifier(),LogisticRegression(),LinearSVC(),KNeighborsClassifier()

        nb.fit(X_train_vect, y_train)
        rf.fit(X_train_vect, y_train)
        lr.fit(X_train_vect, y_train)
        svc.fit(X_train_vect, y_train)
        knn.fit(X_train_vect, y_train)



        ynb_pred = nb.predict(X_test_vect)
        yrf_pred = rf.predict(X_test_vect)
        ylog_pred = log.predict(X_test_vect)
        ysvm_pred = svc.predict(X_test_vect)
        yknn_pred = knn.predict(X_test_vect)


        print("Multinomial naive bayes = ",accuracy_score(testy,ynb_pred))
        print("Random forest = ",accuracy_score(y_test,yrf_pred))
        print("Logistic regression = ",accuracy_score(y_test,ylog_pred))
        print("Support Vector Classifier = ",accuracy_score(y_test,ysvm_pred))
        print("K-Nearest Neighbor = ",accuracy_score(y_test,yknn_pred))
```

Figure 5.31Fit the data with NB, LR, RF, SVM and KNN Classifier.

```
In [80]: import numpy as np
         movie_reviews_array=np.array(["""જો કોઇ સમીક્ષક ચાહે તો ટોટલ ધમાલના ધજાગરા ઉડાવી શકે છે પણ એ કરવુ સારુ નહી રહે.
                                         કારણ કે બધાને ખબર છે કે ફિલ્મના અભિનેતા શુ કરી રહ્યા છે અને નિર્દેશક કેવા પ્રકારની ફિલ્મ બનાવી રહ્યા છે.
                                         આ સાચુ છે કે કેટલાક સીસ તમને લાગશે કે બળજબરીથી હસાવવા માટે નાખી દીધા છે પણ એ પણ છે કે ખાલી
                                         મગજથી જો તમે આ ફિલ્મ જોશો તો તમારા ચેહરા પર હાસ્ય બની રહેશે. આ ફિલ્મને જોવાની સૌથી સારી રીત છે
                                         કે તમે તમારા બાળકો સાથે જાવ. કદાચ તમારા બાળકોની સ્માઇલ જોઇને તમારા પૈસા વસૂલ થઇ જશે."""])

         movie_review_vector = vect.transform(movie_reviews_array)

         review = nb.predict(movie_review_vector)

         if review<=0:
             print("movie is not that good")
         else:
             print("movie is good")

         movie is not that good

In [81]: movie_reviews_array=np.array(["""સુપર હીરોઝને જો આપણે એક યૂનિવર્સલ અપીલના રૂપમાં જોઇએ તો ખોટુ નહી રહે. તેમની જાંબાજીના કારનામા
                                         અને અદ્દભૂત અનોખી શક્તિઓએ સમય સમય પર વિશ્વને બચાવ્યુ"""])

         movie_review_vector = vect.transform(movie_reviews_array)

         review = nb.predict(movie_review_vector)

         if review<=0:
             print("movie is not that good")
         else:
             print("movie is good")

         movie is good
```

Figure 5.32 GMLSA sentiment prediction output.

5.4 Evaluation Matrix

A confusion matrix is generated for performance evaluation using a sentiment calculation technique with five independent datasets. The accuracy, precision, recall, and f1 score based on the confusion matrix are constructed for performance assessment using the proposed algorithms on movie reviews (96,136,152). Figure 5.33 represents the definition created to plot confusion matrix visually.

```
In [4]:
def plot_matrix(matrix,name):
    cf_matrix = matrix
    print(cf_matrix)

    group_names = ['True Neg','False Pos','False Neg','True Pos']

    group_counts = ["{0:0.0f}".format(value) for value in
                    cf_matrix.flatten()]

    group_percentages = ["{0:.2%}".format(value) for value in
                         cf_matrix.flatten()/np.sum(cf_matrix)]

    labels = [f"{v1}\n{v2}\n{v3}" for v1, v2, v3 in
              zip(group_names,group_counts,group_percentages)]

    labels = np.asarray(labels).reshape(2,2)

    ax = sns.heatmap(cf_matrix, annot=labels, fmt='', cmap='Blues')

    ax.set_title('Gujweb review Confusion Matrix for ' + name +'\n\n');
    ax.set_xlabel('\nPredicted Values')
    ax.set_ylabel('Actual Values ');

    ## Ticket labels - List must be in alphabetical order
    ax.xaxis.set_ticklabels(['False','True'])
    ax.yaxis.set_ticklabels(['False','True'])

    ## Display the visualization of the Confusion Matrix.
    plt.show()
```

Figure 5.33 Plotting confusion matrix

The quality of a statistical or machine learning model may be measured using evaluation metrics. Any project requires a thorough examination of machine learning models and methods. To test a model, you may use a variety of assessment measures. Author has used f1-score, accuracy, precision and recall as performance evaluation criteria (12) (21).

Assessment measurements can be used to estimate the nature of a factual or AI model. Any business necessitates a thorough examination of AI models and techniques. You can use a variety of evaluation measures to test a model. As execution assessment models, the creator has used f1-score, exactness, correctness, and recall (136-138) (155).

5.4.1 Accuracy

The most frequently involved measurement for assessing a model, but it's anything but a dependable indicator of its presentation. At the point when courses are unequal, the circumstance turns out to be far more terrible (155).

$$Accuracy = \frac{True\ Positive + True\ Negative}{True\ Positive + False\ Positive + False\ Negative + True\ Negative}$$

(3)

Consider the instance of a disease discovery model. The chances of creating disease are very thin. We should accept that out of 100 patients, 90 don't have malignant growth and the leftover ten have. We would rather not neglect a patient who is experiencing malignant growth yet is slipping through the cracks (bogus negative). The precision of distinguishing everybody as not having disease is 90%. For this situation, the model just determined that each of the 100 expectations would be sans disease.

5.4.2 Precision

Positive occurrences as a percentage of all anticipated positive events. The denominator is the model expectation derived from the entire dataset (155). Consider it a test to determine "how much the model is correct when it claims to be correct."

$$Precision = \frac{True\ Positive}{True\ Positive + False\ Positive}$$

(4)

5.4.3 Recall

Positive rates as a level of the general number of positive occurrences. Subsequently, the numerator (TP + FN) addresses the complete number of positive cases in the assortment (155). Except for the time being that you're attempting to sort out 'the number of additional right ones the model missed when it that introduced the right ones.'

$$recall = \frac{True\ Positive}{True\ Posotive + False\ Negative} \quad (5)$$

5.4.4 F- Score

The mean of accuracy and review is symphonic. This variable considers both, therefore the higher the F1 score, the better. As may be expected, if one's numerator score falls below a certain threshold, one's F1 score falls precipitously. So, if the expected up-sides are certain up-sides (exactness), and the model does not pass up-sides and estimates them negative, it performs well in the F1 score (review) (155).

$$F1\ Score = 2 * \frac{Recall * Precision}{Recall + Precision} \tag{6}$$

6. RESULTS

In terms of execution, the proposed frameworks are put to the test, with the split proportion utilised to select the preparation and test sets. According to the study, the Machine learning-based framework performs better on average, with 70% of informational collection going toward preparing informational collection and 30% going toward evaluating informative index. The results show a considerable improvement after pre-processing the underlying surveys, showing that major discoveries have been discovered (136-138).

Table 5.1 lists the five separate datasets created for these studies. These datasets are pre-processed to balance them and offer more accurate results. Some of the assessment measures used are correctness, precision, recalls, and the f-measure. GujaratiSentiwordnet was created to put to the test a suggested lexicon-based architecture for categorising positive and negative sentiment in reviews. GujaratiSentiWordNet is used to evaluate the proposed method, which recognises and categorises each movie's feelings as 0 (negative) or 1 (positive). Table 6.1 shows the exactness, accuracy, recall, and f-score obtained by the lexicon-based approach using movie review datasets. According to Figure 6.6, the accuracy scores are good, and GujaratiSentiWordNet could be used as a benchmark (133).

The suggested AI-based system is put to the test, with the preparation and test sets determined by the split rate. In general, the system works better, with 70% of the information being prepared and 30% being tested. Five different classifiers are used to examine five different datasets. Table 6.2 exhibits the exactness correlation of five different classifiers on different datasets using TF-IDF and CV as element selection. Except for KNN, all classifiers perform admirably on varied datasets, with precision above 75%. Figure 6.6 shows an overview of the effectiveness-based correlation of classifiers. Except for KNN, all classifiers perform brilliantly on diverse datasets, with accuracy above 75% (134,135).

With datasets from Hungama, Times of India, and Filmfare, the ML-based technique outperforms the vocabulary-based methods by 10%. On datasets like user and Gujwebiduniya, the two approaches get nearly identical results.

6.1 Gujarati text lexicon-based sentiment analysis (GLSA)

GujaratiSentiwordnet created for evaluation of lexicon based proposed architecture to classify sentiment of reviews in to positive and negative. Resource-based classification technique is used with GujaratiSentiWordNet for evaluating proposed method which identify sentiments of each movie and classified into 0(Negative) and 1(Positive).

Gujarati sentiment vocabulary approach is applied on five different dataset and results are generated based on sentiment score. exactness, accuracy, recall, and f-score are the evaluation criteria to measure performance of this proposed algorithm. As demonstrated in Table 6.1, utilising GujaratiSentiwordNet, author able to achieve an average precision, recall, f1-score, and accuracy of 50 percent plus. According to Figure 6.6, the accuracy scores are satisfactory, and GujaratiSentiWordNet might be used as a benchmark.

The accuracy, precision, recall, and f1 score based on the confusion matrix are constructed for performance assessment using the proposed lexicon-based sentiment calculation algorithm on movie reviews collected from the different movie review site. For the Filmfare dataset, the suggested technique has a 62.62 percent accuracy rate. For the Hungama dataset, the suggested technique has a

63.98 percent accuracy rate. For the Times of India dataset, the suggested technique has a 63.98 percent accuracy rate. For the User dataset, the suggested technique has a 53.58 percent accuracy rate. For the Gujweb dataset, the suggested technique has a 58.18 percent accuracy rate.

Figure 6.1 depicts the Gujweb dataset's confusion matrix produced from movie reviews obtained from the Gujarati webdunia website. The y axis of the created confusion matrix represents the actual values, while the x axis represents the expected values. After using the GLSA suggested algorithm, There are 61 real negative reviews (TN), 58 inaccurate positive (FP) reviews, 39 fake negative reviews (FN), and 74 honestly optimistic reviews (TP). On this dataset, the GLSA algorithm achieved an overall accuracy of 58.18 percent.

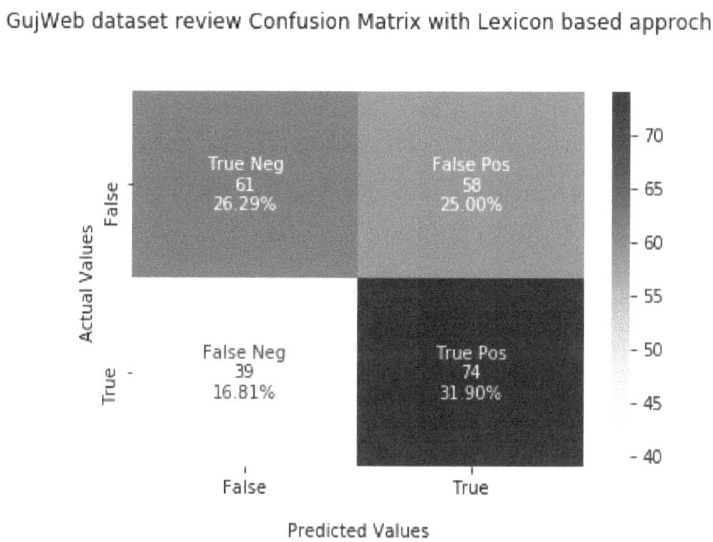

Figure 6.1 Confusion matrix produced by the GLSA algorithm on the evaluation of the GujWeb dataset

The Filmfare dataset uses movie reviews obtained from the Filmfare website to produce a confusion matrix, as shown in Figure 6.2. The y axis of the created confusion matrix represents the actual values, while the x axis represents the expected values. The GLSA-recommended method classifies 18 reviews as real negative, 28 as fake positive, 120 as false negative, and 230 as genuine positive.

On this dataset, the GLSA algorithm achieved an overall accuracy of 62.52 percent.

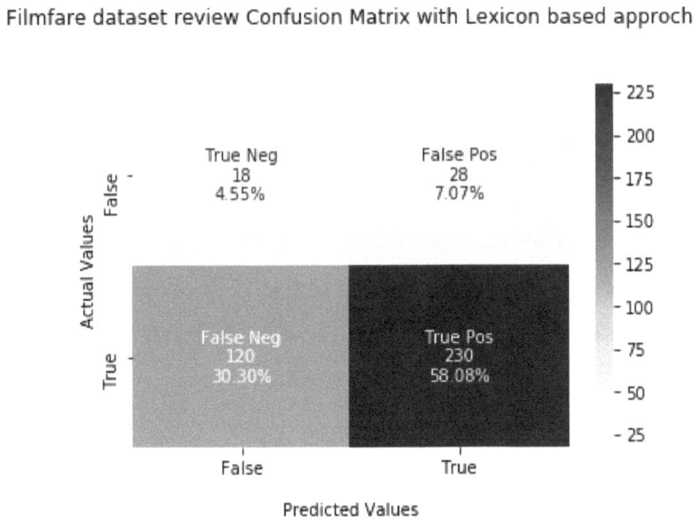

Figure 6.2 Confusion matrix produced by the GLSA algorithm on the evaluation of the FilmFare dataset

Movie reviews were obtained from the Hungama film review website, and the confusion matrix is shown in Figure 6.3. The y axis of the created confusion matrix represents the actual values, while the x axis represents the expected values. 152 reviews are classified as true negative, 143 as false positive, 63 as fake negative, and 214 as genuine positive using the GLSA-recommended approach. With this dataset, the GLSA algorithm achieved an overall accuracy of 63.98 percent.

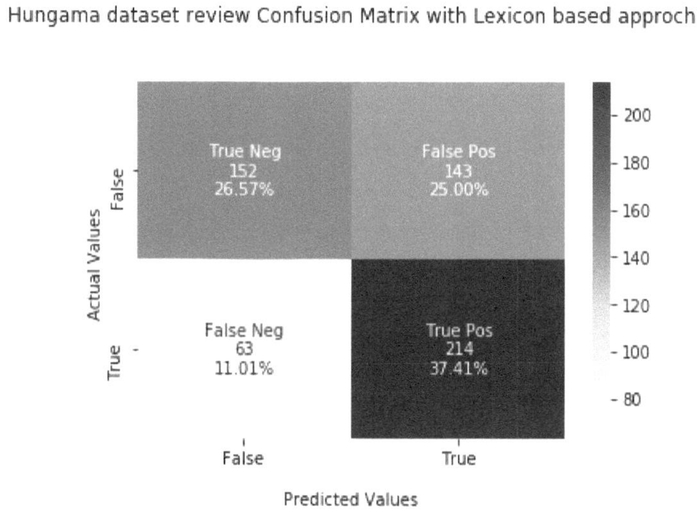

Figure 6.3 Confusion matrix produced by the GLSA algorithm on the evaluation of the Hungama dataset

As shown in Figure 6.4, the TOI dataset uses ratings and reviews from the TimesofIndia film review website to produce a confusion matrix. The resulting confusion matrix's y axis represents the actual values, while the x axis represents the expected values. Using the GLSA-recommended approach, 152 reviews are classified as true negative, 143 as false positive, 63 as false negative, and 214 as genuine positive. The GLSA algorithm has an overall accuracy of 63.98 percent on this dataset.

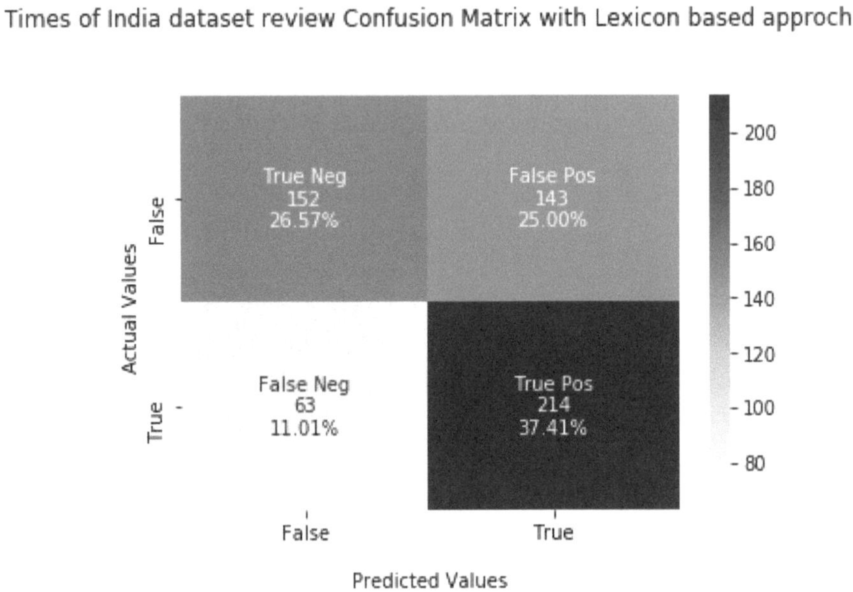

Figure 6.4 Confusion matrix produced by the GLSA algorithm on the evaluation of the Times of India dataset

The User dataset creates a confusion matrix (shown in Figure 6.5) based on user-submitted ratings and comments on movies. The y axis of the created confusion matrix represents the actual values, while the x axis represents the expected values. The GLSA-recommended method classifies 42 reviews as real negative, 56 as false positive, 180 as false negative, and 115 as genuine positive. The GLSA algorithm achieved an overall accuracy of 53.58 percent on this dataset.

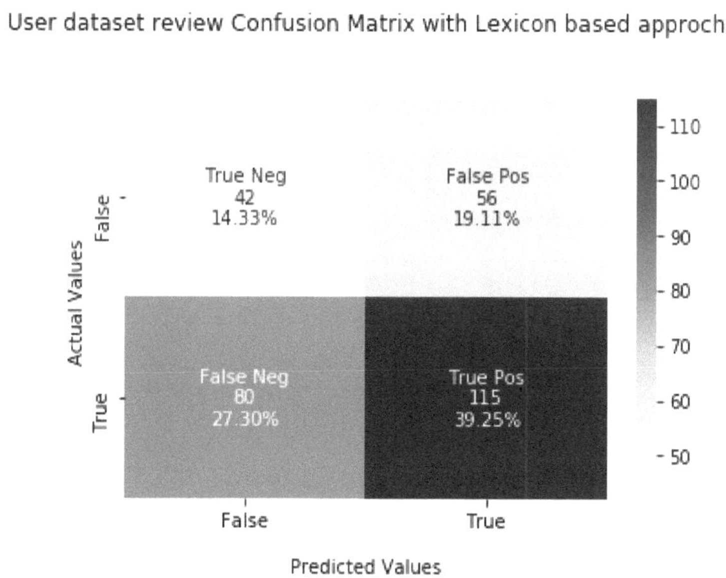

Figure 6.5 Confusion matrix produced by the GLSA algorithm on the evaluation of the User dataset

Table 6.1 The GLSA approach produced a result based on the sentiment score.

Dataset Name	Accuracy (%)	Precision (%)	Recall (%)	F1-score (%)
Gujwebiduniya	58.18	56.06	65.48	60.4
Hungama	63.98	59.94	77.25	67.5
Times of India	63.98	59.94	77.25	67.5
User	53.58	67.25	58.47	62.84
FilmFare	62.62	89.14	65.71	75.65

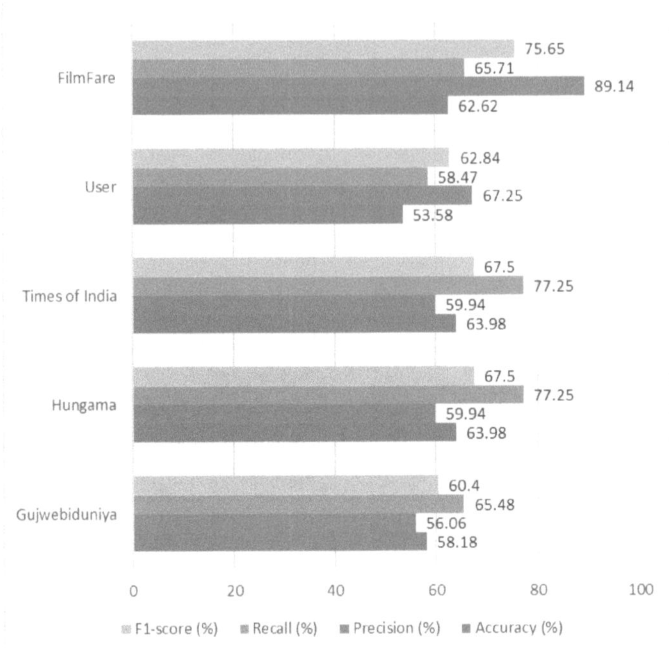

Figure 6.6 The GLSA approach Analysis and evaluation.

6.2 Gujarati text machine learning based sentiment analysis (GMLSA)

The proposed structure is validated for execution by dividing the preparation and test sets according to the split rate. In general, the system outperforms, with 70 percentage of training data and 30 percentage of testing information.

Five unique classifiers are considered on five separate datasets. Table 6.2 compares the precision of five different classifiers on different datasets using TF-IDF and CV as component selection. Aside from KNN, all classifiers perform brilliantly on multiple datasets and provide precision more than 75%. Figure 6.57 depicts a diagram of an exactness-based correlation of classifiers.

Tables 6.3-6.8 examine the exactness, accuracy, review, and f-score of five distinct classifiers on various datasets utilising TF-IDF and CV as component determination methods. Apart from KNN, all classifiers perform well on different datasets, with exactness, accuracy, review, and f-scores over 75%. Figures 6.58-

6.62 depict a graphical evaluation of the exactness, accuracy, review, and f-score of all classifiers based on datasets.

N x N The efficiency of a classification model may be measured with a confusion matrix of N by N columns, where N is the number of classes being measured. Predictions made by the machine learning model are compared to the matrix's true target values. This will allow us to fully see how well our classification model is doing and what kinds of mistakes it is making.

A total of five supervised learning models are deployed to learn sentiments from data. Each model is tested on five distinct datasets before it can be considered complete. Several measures, including F1 score, Accuracy score, Precision, and Recall. Our model's efficacy was evaluated using a Confusion Matrix.

88.57%, 82.86, 85.71%, 88.57%, and 67.14% accuracy were produced on the Gujweb dataset by the NB, RF, LR, SVM, and KNN classifiers, respectively, to pick features by use of the TF-IDF method.

Figure 6.7 shows the confusion matrix made by a naive Bayesian classifier using TF-IDF to choose features on the Gujweb dataset of movie reviews from the Gujarati webidunia review website. The y axis of the created confusion matrix represents the actual values, while the x axis represents the expected values. 35 reviews are classified as real negative, 0 as false positive, 8 as fake negative, and 27 as genuine positive using the GMLSA-recommended approach. With this dataset, the GMLSA algorithm achieved an overall accuracy of 88.57 percent.

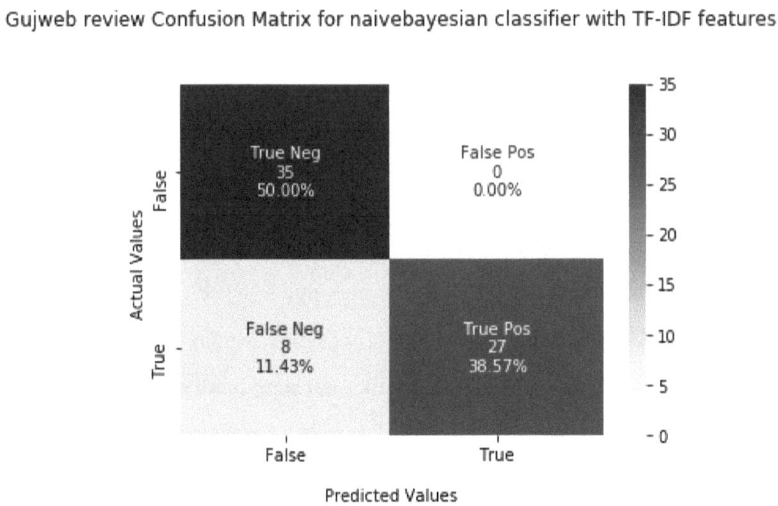

Figure 6.7 Confusion matrix for Gujweb review using a naïve Bayesian classifier and TF-IDF

The confusion matrix constructed by the RF classifier using TF-IDF as feature selection on the Gujweb dataset movie reviews obtained from the Gujarati webidunia review website is shown in Figure 6.8. The y axis of the created confusion matrix represents the actual values, while the x axis represents the expected values. The GMLSA-recommended method classifies 29 reviews as real negative, 6 as false positive, 6 as false negative, and 29 as genuine positive. On this dataset, the GMLSA algorithm achieved an overall accuracy of 82.86 percent.

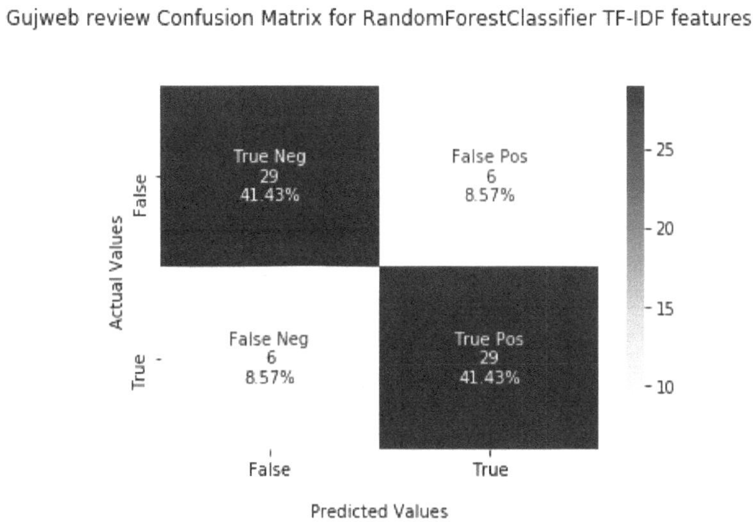

Figure 6.8 Confusion matrix for Gujweb review using a Random Forest classifier and TF-IDF

The confusion matrix constructed by the LR classifier using TF-IDF as feature selection on the Gujweb dataset shown in Figure 6.9. The y axis of the created confusion matrix represents the actual values, while the x axis represents the expected values. The GMLSA-recommended method classifies 31 reviews as real negative, 4 as false positive, 6 as fake negative, and 29 as genuine positive. The GMLSA algorithm achieved an overall accuracy of 85.71 percent on this dataset.

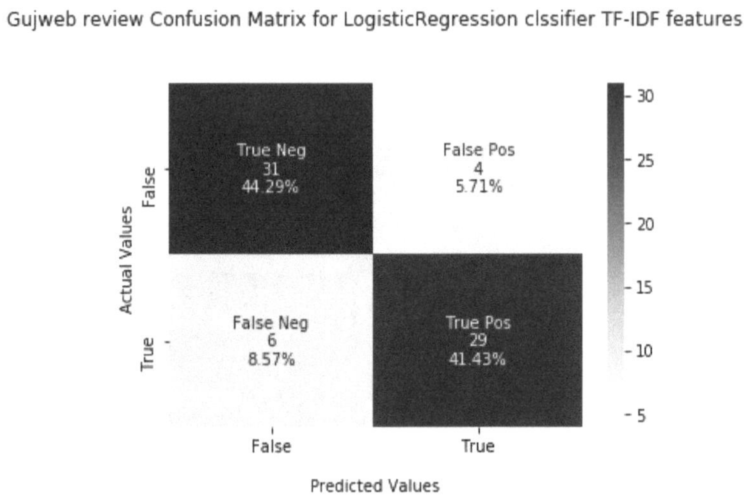

Figure 6.9 Confusion matrix for Gujweb review using a Logistic Regression classifier and TF-IDF

The confusion matrix built by the SVM classifier with TF-IDF as feature selection on the Gujweb dataset movie reviews obtained from the Gujarati webidunia review website is shown in Figure 6.10. The y axis of the created confusion matrix represents the actual values, while the x axis represents the expected values. The GMLSA-recommended method classifies 31 reviews as real negative, 4 as false positive, 4 as fake negative, and 31 as genuine positive. On this dataset, the GMLSA algorithm achieved an overall accuracy of 88.57 percent.

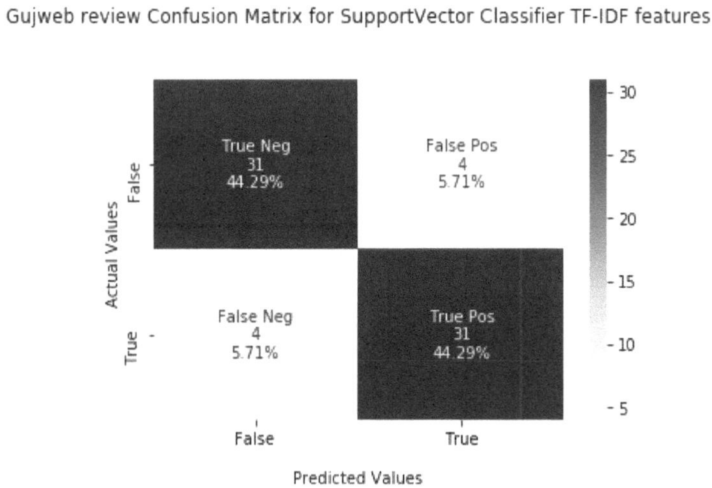

Figure 6.10 Confusion matrix for Gujweb review using a Support Vector classifier and TF-IDF

The confusion matrix created by the KNN classifier using TF-IDF as feature selection on the Gujweb dataset is shown in Figure 6.11. The y axis of the created confusion matrix represents the actual values, while the x axis represents the expected values. 25 evaluations are classified as real negative, 10 as false positive, 13 as fake negative, and 22 as genuine positive using the GMLSA-recommended approach. With this dataset, the GMLSA algorithm achieved an overall accuracy of 67.14 percent.

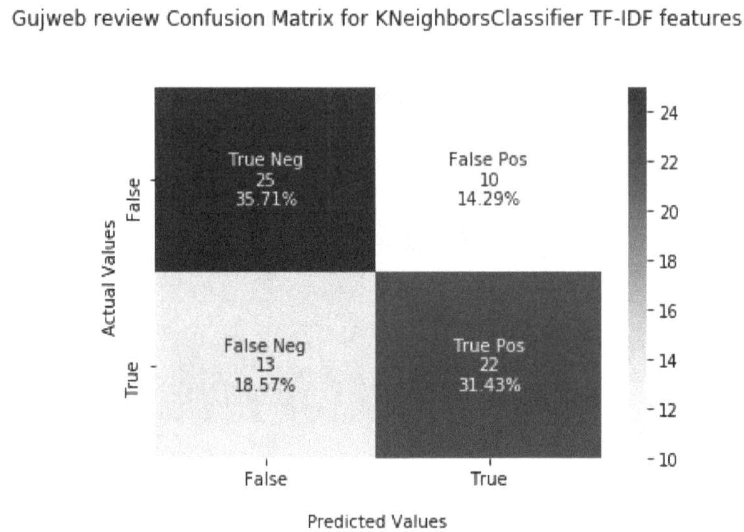

Figure 6.11 Confusion matrix for Gujweb review using a K nearest neighbour classifier and TF-IDF

89.8%, 73.47%, 79.59%, 81.63%, and 71.43% accuracy were produced on the Gujweb dataset by the NB, RF, LR, SVM, and KNN classifiers, respectively, using the feature selection technique CV.

Figure 6.12 illustrates the confusion matrix generated using NB classifier with CV as feature selection on the Gujweb dataset movie reviews acquired from the Gujarati webidunia review website. The y axis of the created confusion matrix represents the actual values, while the x axis represents the expected values. The GMLSA-recommended method classifies 16 reviews as real negative, 0 as false positive, 5 as fake negative, and 28 as genuine positive. The GMLSA algorithm achieved an overall accuracy of 89.8 percent on this dataset.

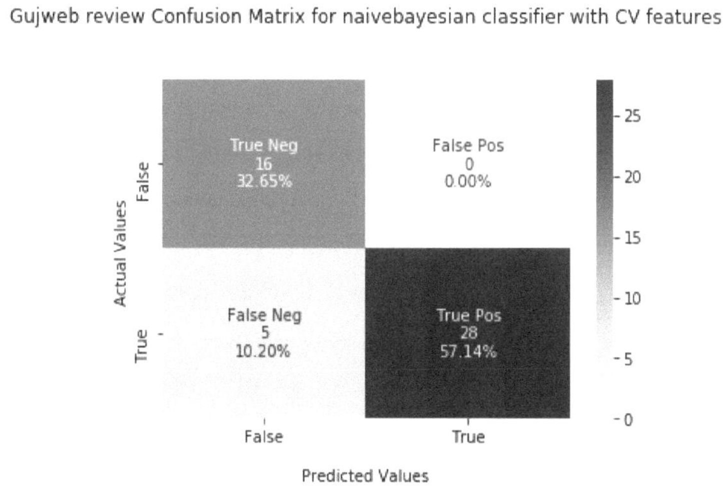

Figure 6.12 Confusion matrix for Gujweb review using a naïve Bayesian classifier and CV

Figure 6.13 illustrates the confusion matrix generated using RF classifier with CV as feature selection on the Gujweb dataset movie reviews acquired from the Gujarati webidunia review website. The y axis of the created confusion matrix represents the actual values, while the x axis represents the expected values. The GMLSA-recommended method classifies 16 reviews as real negative, 0 as false positive, 13 as fake negative, and 20 as genuine positive. On this dataset, the GMLSA algorithm achieved an overall accuracy of 73.47 percent.

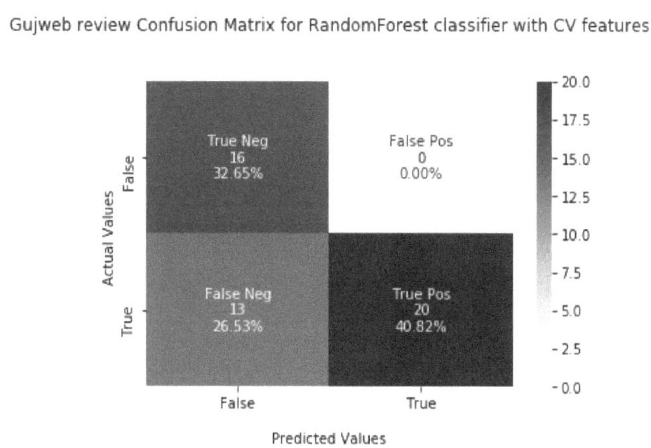

Figure 6.13 Confusion matrix for Gujweb review using a Random Forest classifier and CV

Figure 6.14 illustrates the confusion matrix generated using LR classifier with CV as feature selection on the Gujweb dataset movie reviews acquired from the Gujarati webidunia review website. The y axis of the created confusion matrix represents the actual values, while the x axis represents the expected values. The GMLSA-recommended approach classifies 12 reviews as real negative, 4 as false positive, 6 as false negative, and 27 as genuine positive. The GMLSA algorithm achieved an overall accuracy of 79.59 percent on this dataset.

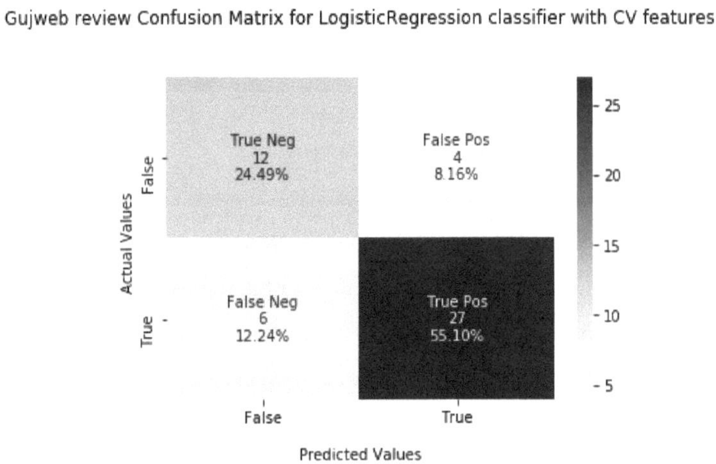

Figure 6.14 Confusion matrix for Gujweb review using a Logistic Regression classifier and CV

Figure 6.15 illustrates the confusion matrix generated using SVM classifier with CV as feature selection on the Gujweb dataset movie reviews acquired from the Gujarati webidunia review website. The y axis of the created confusion matrix represents the actual values, while the x axis represents the expected values. The GMLSA-recommended approach classifies 13 evaluations as real negative, 3 as false positive, 6 as false negative, and 27 as genuine positive. With this dataset, the GMLSA algorithm achieved an overall accuracy of 81.63 percent.

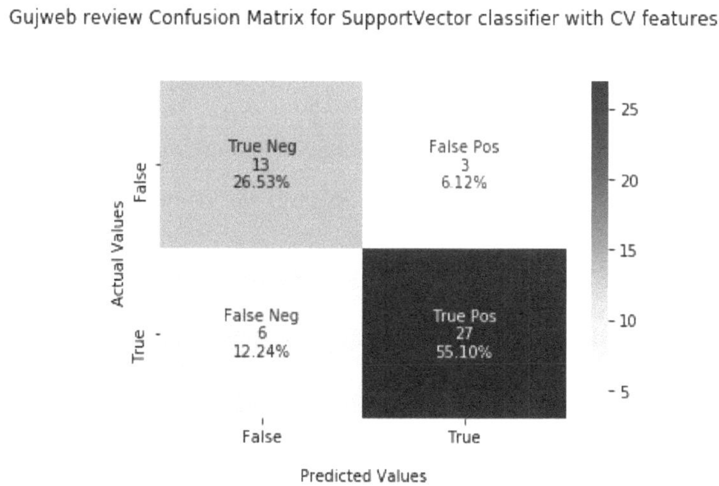

Figure 6.15 Confusion matrix for Gujweb review using a Support Vector classifier and CV

Figure 6.16 illustrates the confusion matrix generated using KNN classifier with CV as feature selection on the Gujweb dataset movie reviews acquired from the Gujarati webidunia review website. The y axis of the created confusion matrix represents the actual values, while the x axis represents the expected values. The GMLSA-recommended method classifies 9 reviews as real negative, 7 as false positive, 7 as false negative, and 26 as genuine positive. The GMLSA algorithm achieved an overall accuracy of 71.43 percent on this dataset.

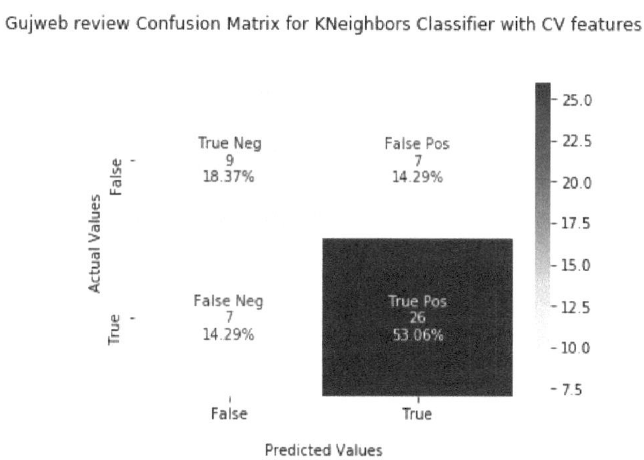

Figure 6.16 Confusion matrix for Gujweb review using a K nearest neighbour classifier and CV

85.71%, 90.48%, 85.71%, 90.48%, and 85.71% accuracy were produced on the Filmfare dataset by the NB, RF, LR, SVM, and KNN classifiers, respectively, using the feature selection technique TF-IDF.

The confusion matrix constructed using the NB classifier with TF-IDF as feature selection on the Filmfare dataset movie reviews obtained from the Filmfare review website is shown in Figure 6.17. The y axis of the created confusion matrix represents the actual values, while the x axis represents the expected values. The GMLSA-recommended method classifies 0 reviews as real negative, 12 as false positive, 0 as fake negative, and 72 as genuine positive. The GMLSA algorithm achieved an overall accuracy of 85.71 percent on this dataset.

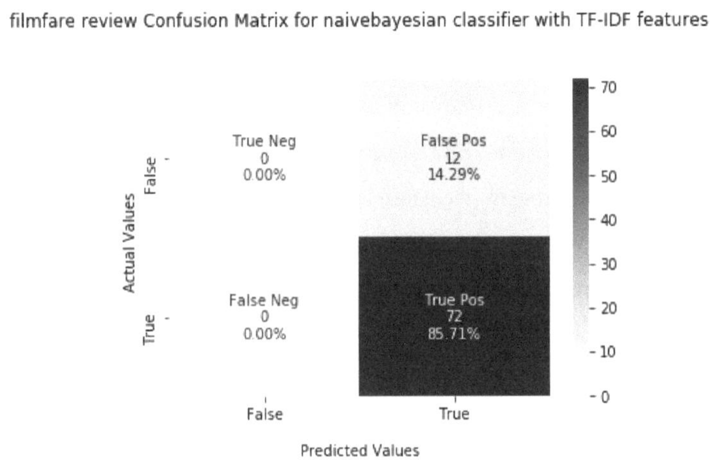

Figure 6.17 Confusion matrix for FilmFare review using a naïve Bayesian classifier and TF-IDF

Figure 6.18 shows the confusion matrix made by the RF classifier with the Filmfare dataset of movie reviews from the Filmfare review site and TF-IDF as a feature selection. The y axis of the created confusion matrix represents the actual values, while the x axis represents the expected values. The GMLSA-recommended approach classifies four reviews as real negative, eight as false positive, zero as false negative, and 72 as genuine positive. With this dataset, the GMLSA algorithm achieved an overall accuracy of 90.48 percent.

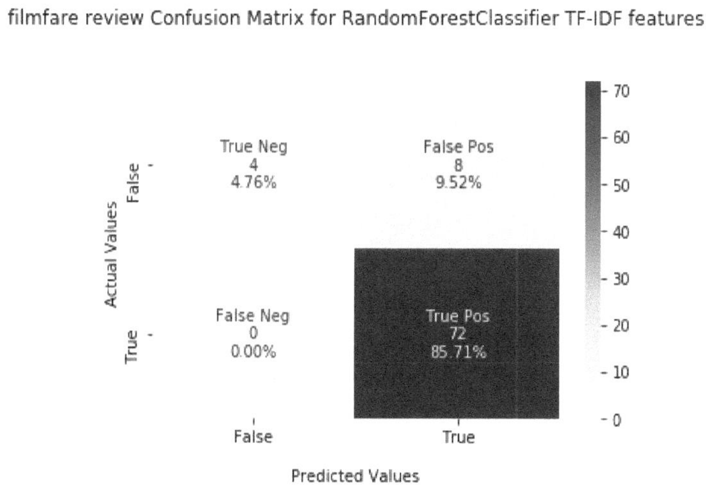

Figure 6.18 Confusion matrix for FilmFare review using a Random Forest classifier and TF-IDF

The website Filmfare.com's movie reviews were used to make a dataset, and Figure 6.19 shows the results of using the LR classifier with TF-IDF as the way to choose features. The y axis of the created confusion matrix represents the actual values, while the x axis represents the expected values. The GMLSA-recommended method classifies 0 reviews as real negative, 12 as false positive, 0 as fake negative, and 72 as genuine positive. On this dataset, the GMLSA algorithm achieved an overall accuracy of 85.71 percent.

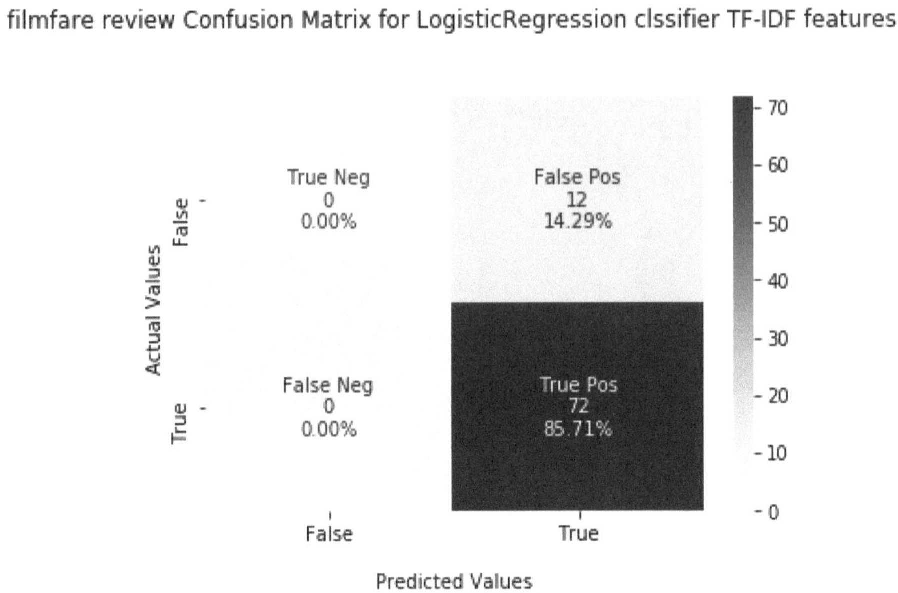

Figure 6.19 Confusion matrix for FilmFare review using a Logistic Regression classifier and TF-IDF

Movie reviews from the Filmfare review website were used to train a support vector machine (SVM) classifier, and the confusion matrix it produced is depicted in Figure 6.20. The SVM classifier used TF-IDF to identify features.The y axis of the created confusion matrix represents the actual values, while the x axis represents the expected values. The GMLSA-recommended approach classifies four reviews as real negative, eight as false positive, zero as false negative, and 72 as genuine positive. With this dataset, the GMLSA algorithm achieved an overall accuracy of 90.48 percent.

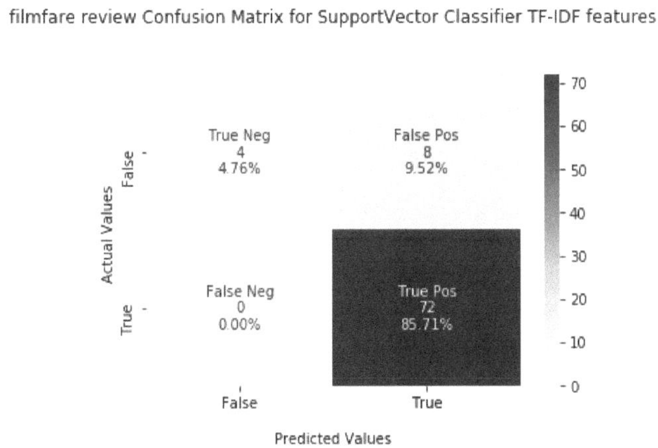

Figure 6.20 Confusion matrix for FilmFare review using a Support Vector classifier and TF-IDF

Figure 6.21 depicts the confusion matrix generated by the KNN classifier using TF-IDF as a feature selection on the Filmfare dataset consisting of movie reviews pulled from the Filmfare review website. The y axis of the created confusion matrix represents the actual values, while the x axis represents the expected values. The GMLSA-recommended method classifies 0 reviews as real negative, 12 as false positive, 0 as fake negative, and 72 as genuine positive. The GMLSA algorithm achieved an overall accuracy of 85.71 percent on this dataset.

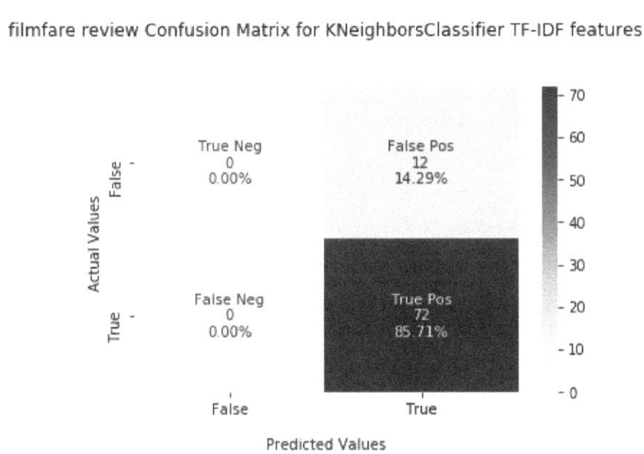

Figure 6.21 Confusion matrix for FilmFare review using a K nearest neighbour classifier and TF-IDF

94.83%, 94.83%, 94.83%, 94.83%, and 65.52% accuracy were produced on the Filmfare dataset by the NB, RF, LR, SVM, and KNN classifiers, respectively, using the feature selection technique CV.

Figure 6.22 illustrates the confusion matrix generated using NB classifier with CV as feature selection on the Filmfare dataset movie reviews acquired from the Filmfare review website. The y axis of the created confusion matrix represents the actual values, while the x axis represents the expected values. The GMLSA-recommended approach classifies two reviews as real negative, three as false positive, zero as false negative, and 53 as genuine positive. With this dataset, the GMLSA algorithm achieved an overall accuracy of 94.83 percent.

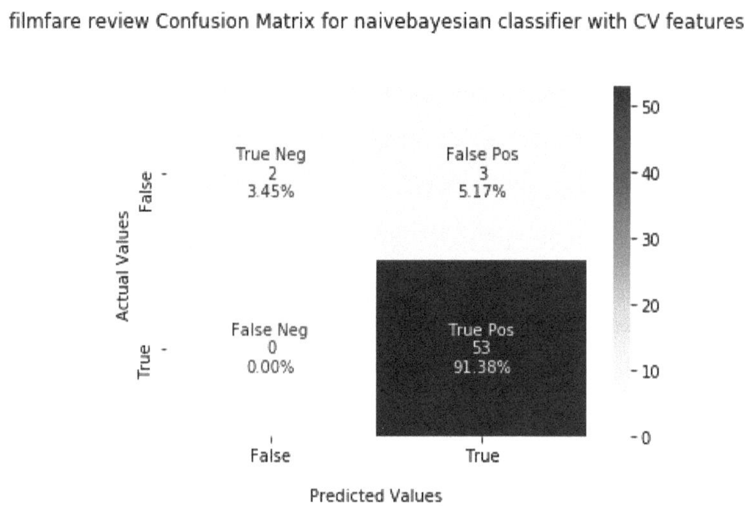

Figure 6.22 Confusion matrix for FilmFare review using a naïve Bayesian classifier and CV

Figure 6.23 illustrates the confusion matrix generated using RF classifier with CV as feature selection on the Filmfare dataset movie reviews acquired from the Filmfare review website. The resulting confusion matrix's y axis represents the actual values, while the x axis represents the expected values. Using the GMLSA-recommended approach, 2 reviews are classified as real negative, 3 as false positive, 0 as false negative, and 53 as genuine positive. The GMLSA algorithm has an overall accuracy of 94.83 percent on this dataset.

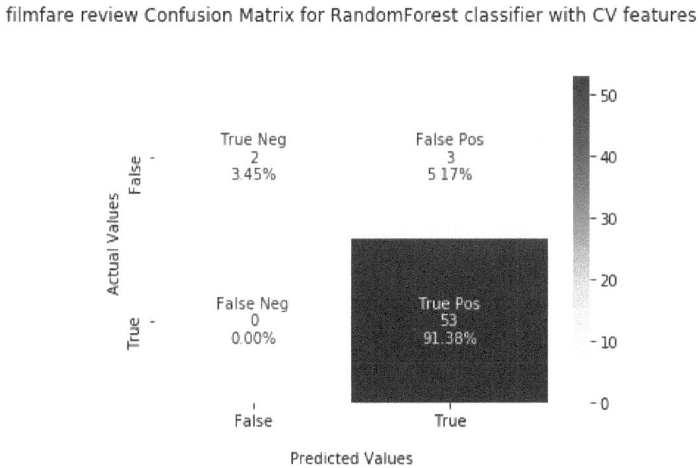

Figure 6.23 Confusion matrix for FilmFare review using a Random Forest classifier and CV

Figure 6.24 illustrates the confusion matrix generated using LR classifier with CV as feature selection on the Filmfare dataset movie reviews acquired from the Filmfare review website. The y axis of the generated confusion matrix represents the actual values, while the x axis represents the expected values. The GMLSA-recommended approach classifies 2 reviews as real negative, 3 as false positive, 0 as fake negative, and 53 as genuine positive. The GMLSA algorithm produced an overall accuracy of 94.83 percent on this dataset.

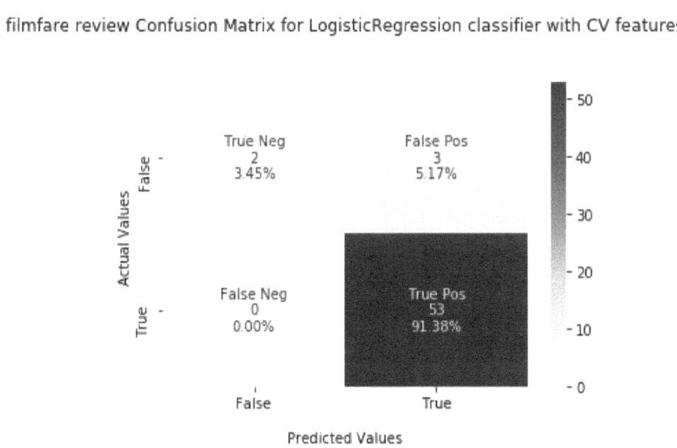

Figure 6.24 Confusion matrix for FilmFare review using a Logistic Regression classifier and CV

Figure 6.25 illustrates the confusion matrix generated using SVM classifier with CV as feature selection on the Filmfare dataset movie reviews acquired from the Filmfare review website. The y axis of the created confusion matrix represents the actual values, while the x axis represents the expected values. The GMLSA-recommended approach classifies two reviews as real negative, three as false positive, zero as false negative, and 53 as genuine positive. With this dataset, the GMLSA algorithm achieved an overall accuracy of 94.83 percent.

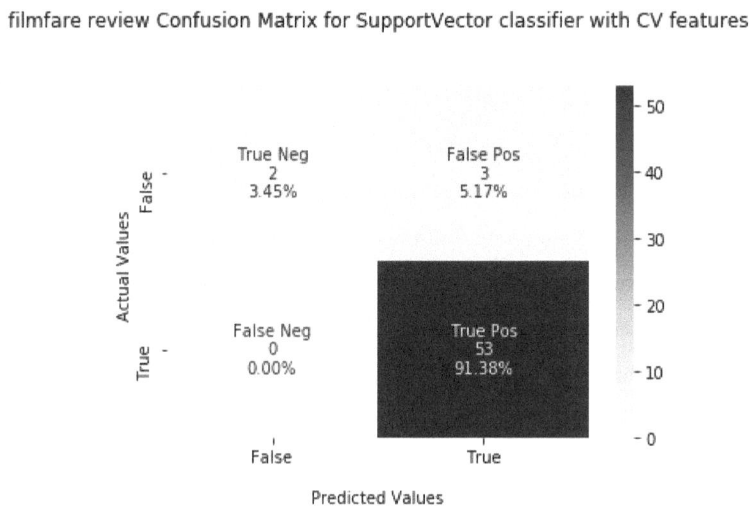

Figure 6.25 Confusion matrix for FilmFare review using a Support Vector classifier and CV

Figure 6.26 illustrates the confusion matrix generated using KNN classifier with CV as feature selection on the Filmfare dataset movie reviews acquired from the Filmfare review website. The y axis of the created confusion matrix represents the actual values, while the x axis represents the expected values. The GMLSA-recommended approach classifies one review as true negative, four as false positive, sixteen as false negative, and 37 as genuine positive. With this dataset, the GMLSA algorithm achieved an overall accuracy of 65.52 percent.

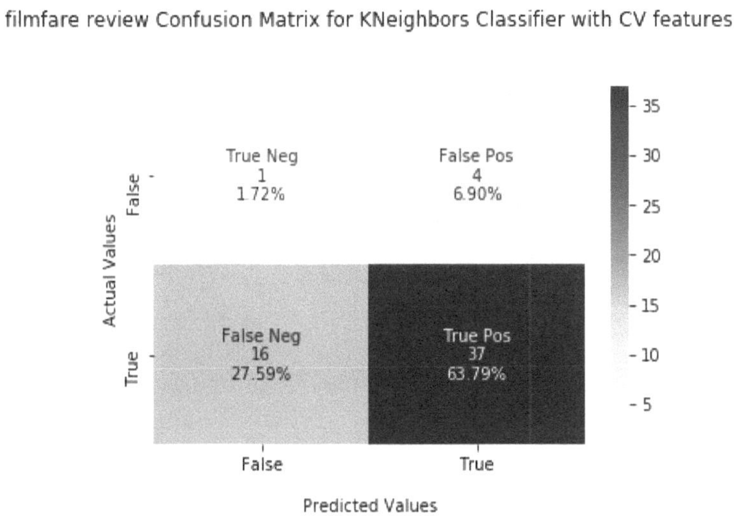

Figure 6.26 Confusion matrix for FilmFare review using a K nearest neighbour classifier and CV

84.83%, 92.13%, 95.51%, 94.38%, and 59.55% accuracy were produced on the Hungama dataset by the NB, RF, LR, SVM, and KNN classifiers, respectively, using the feature selection technique TF-IDF.

The confusion matrix constructed using the NB classifier with TF-IDF as feature selection on the Hungama

Dataset is shown in Figure 6.27. The y axis of the created confusion matrix represents the actual values, while the x axis represents the expected values. 58 reviews are classified as real negative, 27 as false positive, 0 as fake negative, and 93 as genuine positive using the GMLSA-recommended approach. With this dataset, the GMLSA algorithm achieved an overall accuracy of 84.83 percent.

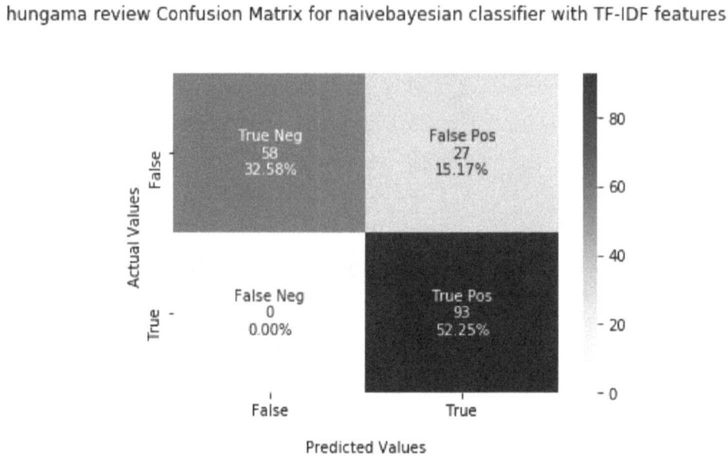

Figure 6.27 Confusion matrix for Hungama review using a naïve Bayesian classifier and TF-IDF

The confusion matrix created by the RF classifier with TF-IDF as feature selection on the Hungama is shown in Figure 6.28. The y axis of the created confusion matrix represents the actual values, while the x axis represents the expected values. 77 evaluations are classified as real negative, 8 as false positive, 6 as fake negative, and 87 as genuine positive using the GMLSA-recommended approach. On this dataset, the GMLSA algorithm achieved an overall accuracy of 92.13 percent.

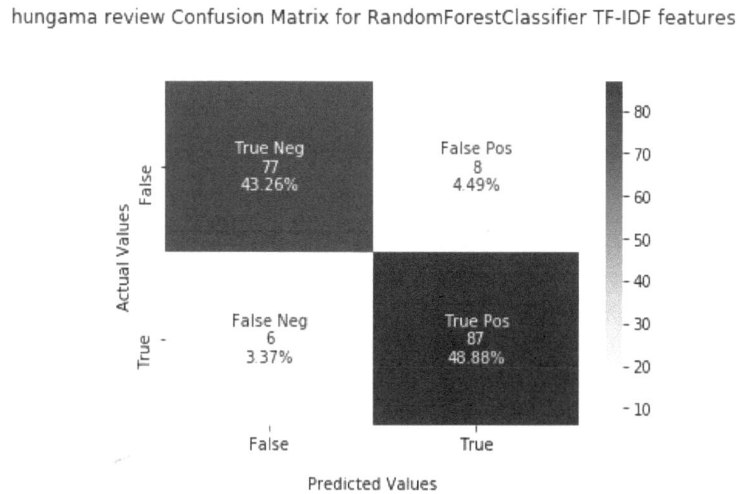

Figure 6.28 Confusion matrix for Hungama review using a Random Forest classifier and TF-IDF

To illustrate this, Figure 6.29 depicts the confusion matrix generated by the LR classifier using TF-IDF as feature selection on the Hungama dataset consisting of movie reviews taken from the Hungama review website. The y axis of the created confusion matrix represents the actual values, while the x axis represents the expected values. 79 evaluations are classified as real negative, 6 as false positive, 2 as fake negative, and 91 as genuine positive using the GMLSA-recommended approach. The GMLSA algorithm achieved an overall accuracy of 95.51 percent on this dataset.

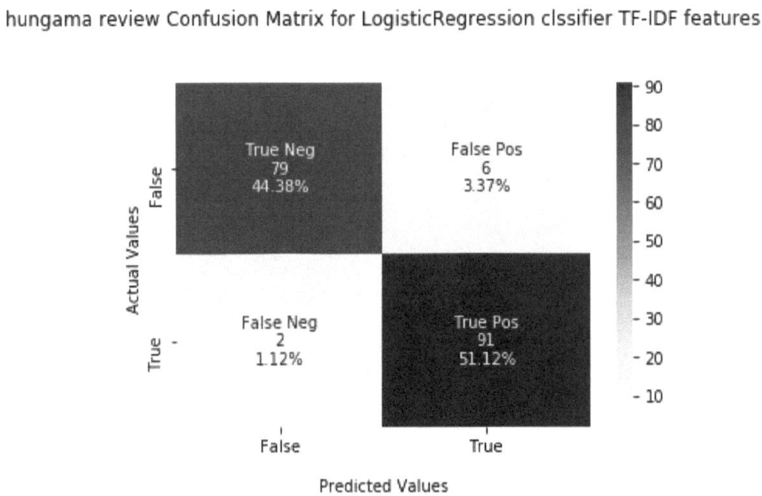

Figure 6.29 Confusion matrix for Hungama review using a Logistic Regression classifier and TF-IDF

In Figure 6.30, we can see the confusion matrix that the SVM classifier made wi th the Hungama dataset, which is made up of movie reviews from the Hungama review website. The y axis of the created confusion matrix represents the actua l values, while the x axis represents the expected values. 79 evaluations are class ified as real negative, 6 as false positive, 4 as fake negative, and 89 as genuine p ositive using the GMLSA-recommended approach. With this dataset, the GML SA algorithm achieved an overall accuracy of 94.38 percent.

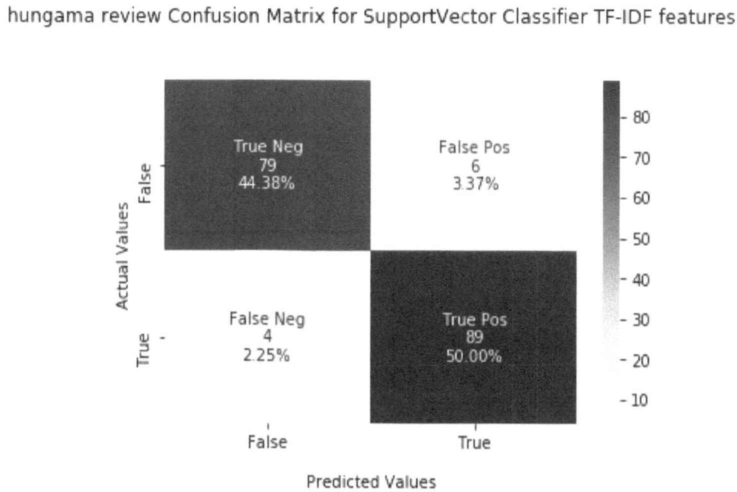

Figure 6.30 Confusion matrix for Hungama review using a Support Vector classifier and TF-IDF

In Figure 6.31, we can see the confusion matrix that the KNN classifier made with the Hungama dataset, which is made up of movie reviews from the Hungama review website. . The y axis of the created confusion matrix represents the actual values, while the x axis represents the expected values. The GMLSA-recommended method classifies 21 reviews as real negative, 64 as false positive, 8 as fake negative, and 85 as genuine positive. On this dataset, the GMLSA algorithm achieved an overall accuracy of 59.54 percent.

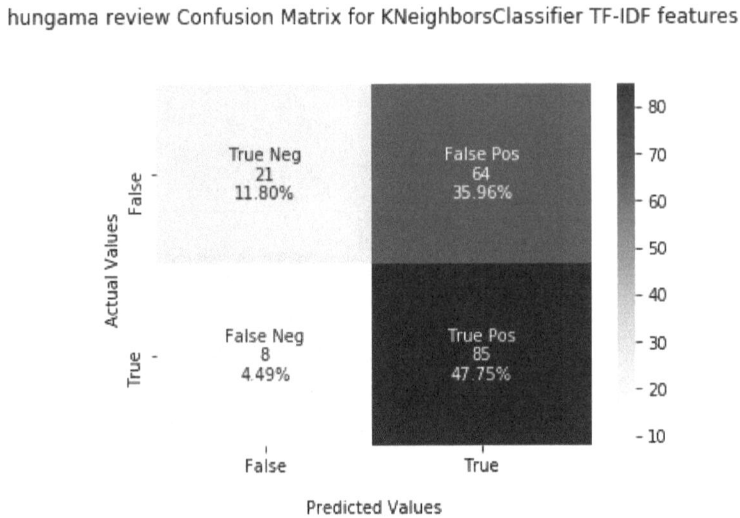

Figure 6.31 Confusion matrix for Hungama review using a K nearest neighbour classifier and TFIDF

81.60%, 82.40%, 84%, 85.6%, and 66.4% accuracy were produced on the Hungama dataset by the NB, RF, LR, SVM, and KNN classifiers, respectively, using the feature selection technique CV.

Figure 6.32 illustrates the confusion matrix generated using NB classifier with CV as feature selection on the Hungama dataset movie reviews acquired from the Hungama review website. The y axis of the created confusion matrix represents the actual values, while the x axis represents the expected values. The GMLSA-recommended method classifies 44 evaluations as real negative, 20 as false positive, 3 as fake negative, and 58 as genuine positive. The GMLSA algorithm achieved an overall accuracy of 81.60 percent on this dataset.

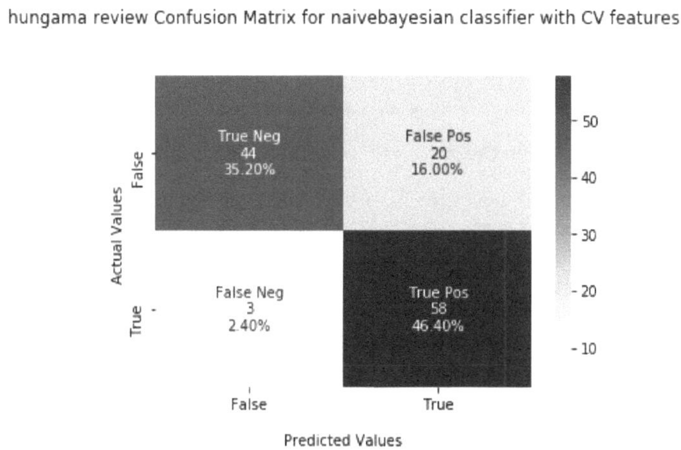

Figure 6.32 Confusion matrix for Hungama review using a naïve Bayesian classifier and CV

Figure 6.33 illustrates the confusion matrix generated using RF classifier with CV as feature selection on the Hungama dataset movie reviews acquired from the Hungama review website. The y axis of the created confusion matrix represents the actual values, while the x axis represents the expected values. The GMLSA-recommended method classifies 46 evaluations as real negative, 18 as false positive, 4 as fake negative, and 57 as genuine positive. With this dataset, the GMLSA algorithm achieved an overall accuracy of 82.40 percent.

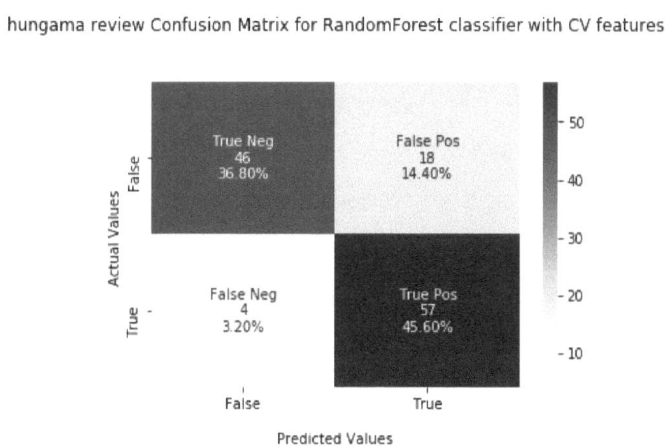

Figure 6.33 Confusion matrix for Hungama review using a Random Forest classifier and CV

Figure 6.34 illustrates the confusion matrix generated using LR classifier with CV as feature selection on the Hungama dataset movie reviews acquired from the Hungama review website. The y axis of the created confusion matrix represents the actual values, while the x axis represents the expected values. The GMLSA-recommended method classifies 52 reviews as real negative, 12 as false positive, 8 as fake negative, and 53 as genuine positive. The GMLSA algorithm achieved an overall accuracy of 84 percent on this dataset.

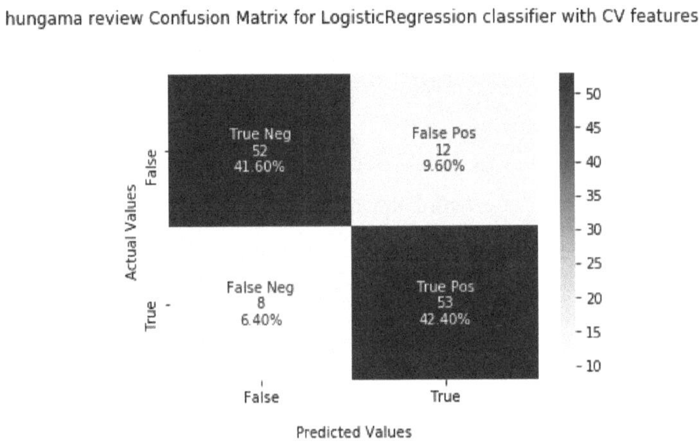

Figure 6.34 Confusion matrix for Hungama review using a Logistic Regression classifier and CV

Figure 6.35 illustrates the confusion matrix generated using SVM classifier with CV as feature selection on the Hungama dataset movie reviews acquired from the Hungama review website. The y axis of the created confusion matrix represents the actual values, while the x axis represents the expected values. The GMLSA-recommended method classifies 52 reviews as real negative, 12 as false positive, 8 as fake negative, and 53 as genuine positive. The GMLSA algorithm achieved an overall accuracy of 85.6 percent on this dataset.

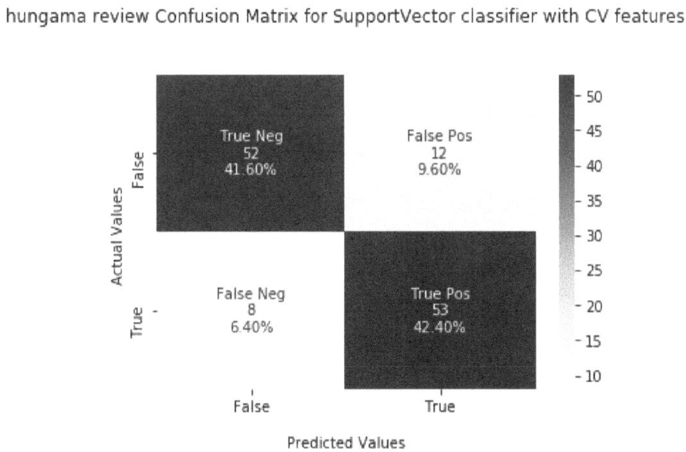

Figure 6.35 Confusion matrix for Hungama review using a Support Vector classifier and CV

Figure 6.36 illustrates the confusion matrix generated using KNN classifier with CV as feature selection on the Hungama dataset movie reviews acquired from the Hungama review website. The y axis of the created confusion matrix represents the actual values, while the x axis represents the expected values. 57 evaluations are classified as real negative, 7 as false positive, 35 as fake negative, and 26 as genuine positive using the GMLSA-recommended approach. The GMLSA algorithm achieved an overall accuracy of 66.4 percent on this dataset.

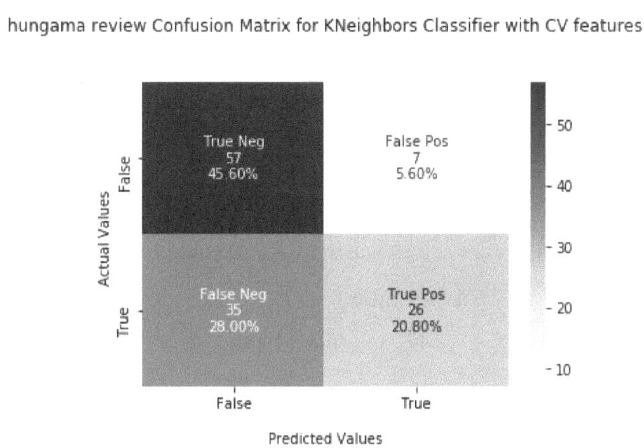

Figure 6.36 Confusion matrix for Hungama review using a K nearest neighbour classifier and CV

94.77%, 93.6%, 94.77%, 94.77%, and 67.44% accuracy were produced on the Times of India dataset by the NB, RF, LR, SVM, and KNN classifiers, respectively, using the feature selection technique TF-IDF.

The confusion matrix constructed using the NB classifier with TF-IDF as feature selection on the TimesofIndia review is shown in Figure 6.37. The y axis of the created confusion matrix represents the actual values, while the x axis represents the expected values. 82 reviews are classified as real negative, 9 as false positive, 0 as fake negative, and 81 as genuine positive using the GMLSA-recommended approach. The GMLSA algorithm achieved an overall accuracy of 94.77 percent on this dataset.

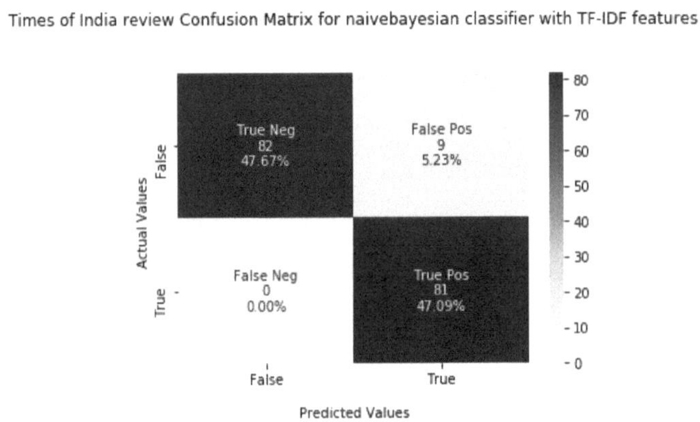

Figure 6.37 Confusion matrix for TOI review using a naïve Bayesian classifier and TF-IDF

The confusion matrix created by the RF classifier with TF-IDF as feature selection on the TOI dataset is shown in Figure 6.38. The y axis of the created confusion matrix represents the actual values, while the x axis represents the expected values. 84 reviews are classified as real negative, 7 as false positive, 4 as fake negative, and 77 as genuine positive using the GMLSA-recommended approach. The GMLSA algorithm achieved an overall accuracy of 93.6 percent on this dataset.

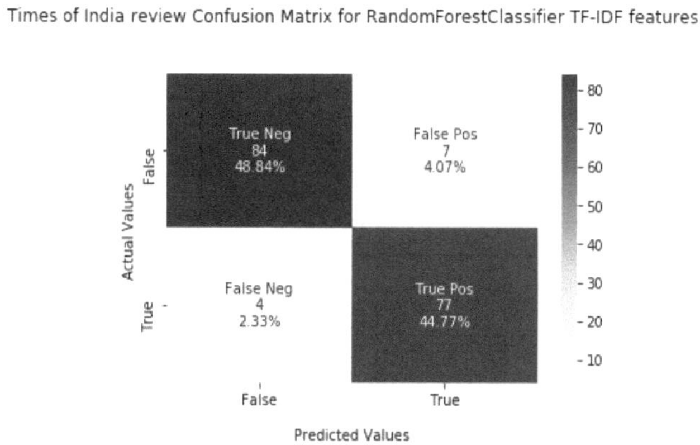

Figure 6.38 Confusion matrix for TOI review using a Random Forest classifier and TF-IDF

The confusion matrix constructed using the LR classifier with TF-IDF as feature selection on the TOI dataset is shown in Figure 6.39. The y axis of the created confusion matrix represents the actual values, while the x axis represents the expected values. 84 reviews are classified as real negative, 7 as false positive, 2 as fake negative, and 79 as genuine positive using the GMLSA-recommended approach. The GMLSA algorithm achieved an overall accuracy of 94.77 percent on this dataset.

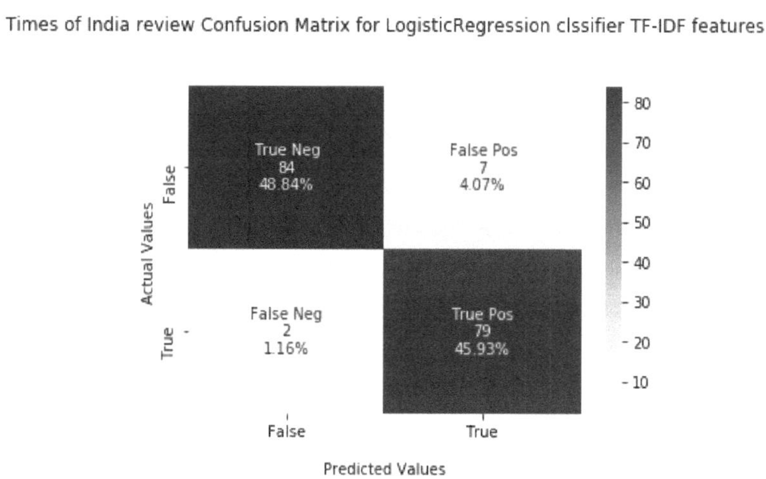

Figure 6.39 Confusion matrix for TOI review using a Logistic Regression classifier and TF-IDF

The confusion matrix created by the SVM classifier with TF-IDF as feature selection on the TOI dataset is shown in Figure 6.40. The y axis of the created confusion matrix represents the actual values, while the x axis represents the expected values. 84 reviews are classified as real negative, 7 as false positive, 2 as fake negative, and 79 as genuine positive using the GMLSA-recommended approach. The GMLSA algorithm achieved an overall accuracy of 94.77 percent on this dataset.

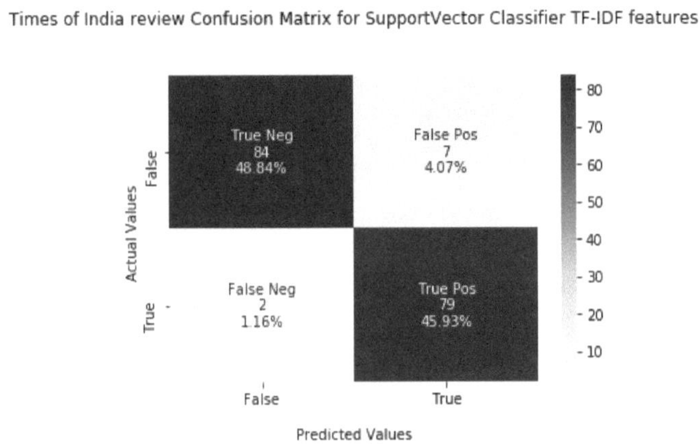

Figure 6.40 Confusion matrix for TOI review using a Support Vector classifier and TF-IDF

The confusion matrix created by the KNN classifier with TF-IDF as feature sele ction on the TOI dataset is shown in Figure 6.41. The y axis of the created confu sion matrix represents the actual values, while the x axis represents the expected values. The GMLSA-recommended method classifies 39 evaluations as real neg ative, 52 as false positive, 4 as fake negative, and 77 as genuine positive. The G MLSA algorithm achieved an overall accuracy of 67.44 percent on this dataset.

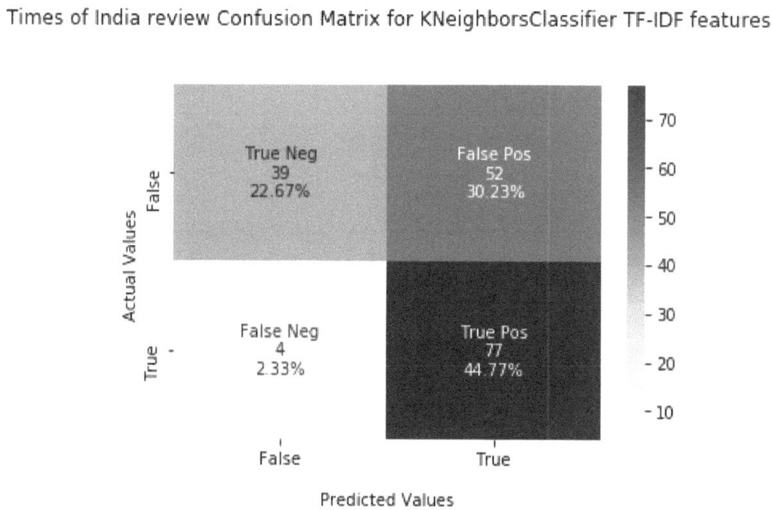

Figure 6.41 Confusion matrix for TOI review using a K nearest neighbour classifier and TF-IDF

91.67%, 89.17%, 90%, 89.17%, and 58.33% accuracy were produced on the Times of India dataset by the NB, RF, LR, SVM, and KNN classifiers, respectively, using the feature selection technique CV.

Figure 6.42 illustrates the confusion matrix generated using NB classifier with CV as feature selection on the TOI dataset movie reviews acquired from the TimesofIndia review website. The y axis of the created confusion matrix represents the actual values, while the x axis represents the expected values. The GMLSA-recommended approach classifies 52 reviews as real negative, 10 as false positive, 0 as false negative, and 58 as genuine positive. The GMLSA algorithm achieved an overall accuracy of 91.67 percent on this dataset.

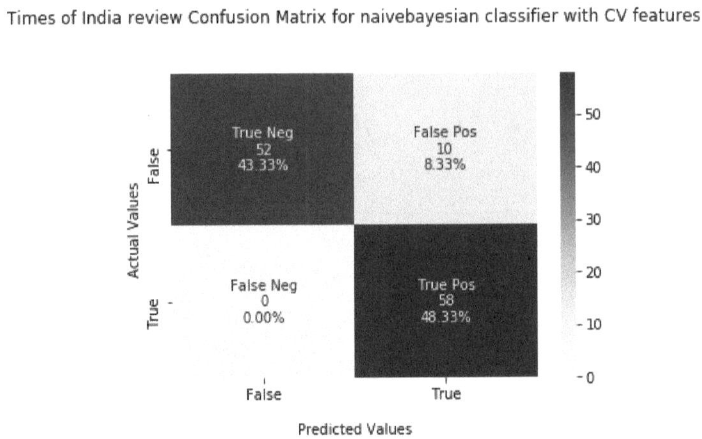

Figure 6.42 Confusion matrix for TOI review using a naïve Bayesian classifier and CV

Figure 6.43 illustrates the confusion matrix generated using RF classifier with CV as feature selection on the TOI dataset movie reviews acquired from the TimesofIndia review website. The y axis of the created confusion matrix represents the actual values, while the x axis represents the expected values. The GMLSA-recommended method classifies 54 reviews as real negative, 8 as false positive, 5 as fake negative, and 53 as genuine positive. The GMLSA algorithm achieved an overall accuracy of 89.17 percent on this dataset.

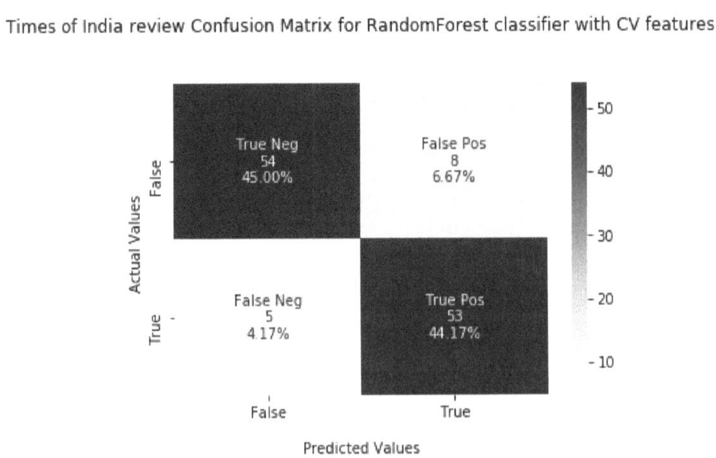

Figure 6.43 Confusion matrix for TOI review using a Random Forest classifier and CV

Figure 6.44 illustrates the confusion matrix generated using LR classifier with CV as feature selection on the TOI dataset movie reviews acquired from the TimesofIndia review website. The y axis of the created confusion matrix represents the actual values, while the x axis represents the expected values. The GMLSA-recommended method classifies 55 reviews as real negative, 7 as false positive, 5 as fake negative, and 53 as genuine positive. On this dataset, the GMLSA algorithm achieved an overall accuracy of 90%.

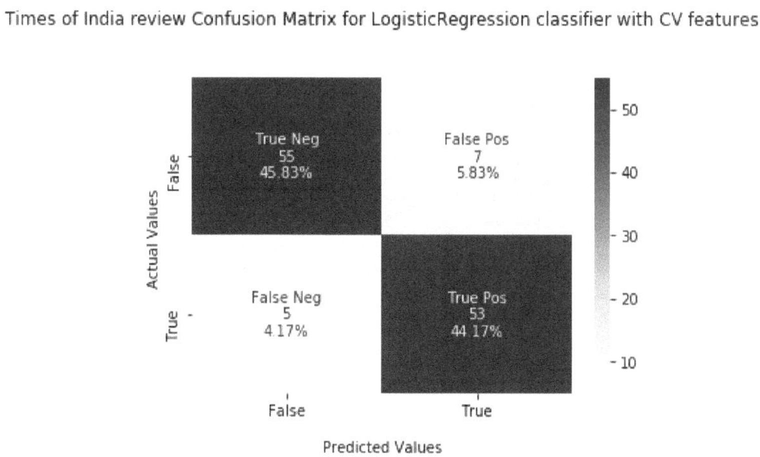

Figure 6.44 Confusion matrix for TOI review using a Logistic Regression classifier and CV

Figure 6.45 illustrates the confusion matrix generated using SVM classifier with CV as feature selection on the TOI dataset movie reviews acquired from the TimesofIndia review website. The y axis of the created confusion matrix represents the actual values, while the x axis represents the expected values. The GMLSA-recommended method classifies 55 reviews as real negative, 7 as false positive, 5 as fake negative, and 53 as genuine positive. The GMLSA algorithm achieved an overall accuracy of 89.17 percent on this dataset.

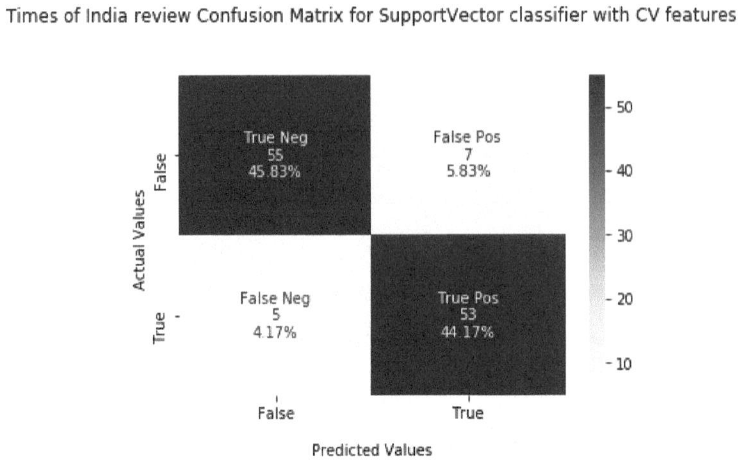

Figure 6.45 Confusion matrix for TOI review using a Support Vector classifier and CV

Figure 6.46 illustrates the confusion matrix generated using KNN classifier with CV as feature selection on the TOI dataset movie reviews acquired from the TimesofIndia review website. The y axis of the created confusion matrix represents the actual values, while the x axis represents the expected values. 62 reviews are classified as real negative, 0 as false positive, 50 as false negative, and 8 as genuine positive using the GMLSA-recommended approach. In this dataset, the GMLSA algorithm achieved an overall accuracy of 58.33 percent.

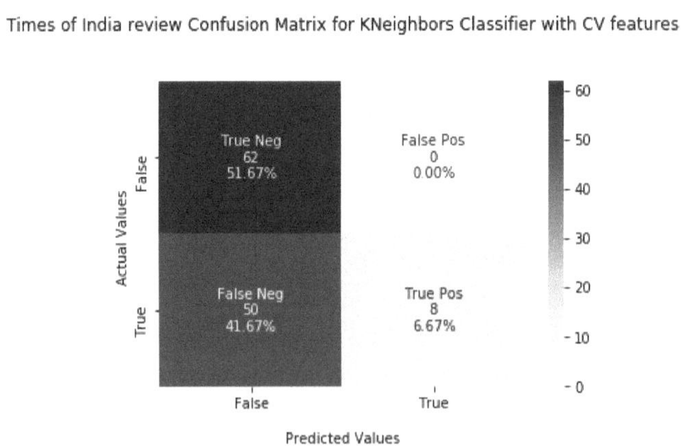

Figure 6.46 Confusion matrix for TOI review using a K nearest neighbour classifier and CV

62.5%, 62.5%, 62.5%, 62.5%, and 64.77% accuracy were produced on the user dataset by the NB, RF, LR, SVM, and KNN classifiers, respectively, using the feature selection technique TF-IDF.

Figure 6.47 depicts the confusion matrix built by the NB classifier using TF-IDF as feature selection on the user dataset. The y axis of the created confusion matrix represents the actual values, while the x axis represents the expected values. The GMLSA-recommended method classifies 0 reviews as real negative, 33 as false positive, 0 as fake negative, and 55 as genuine positive. The GMLSA algorithm achieved an overall accuracy of 62.5 percent on this dataset.

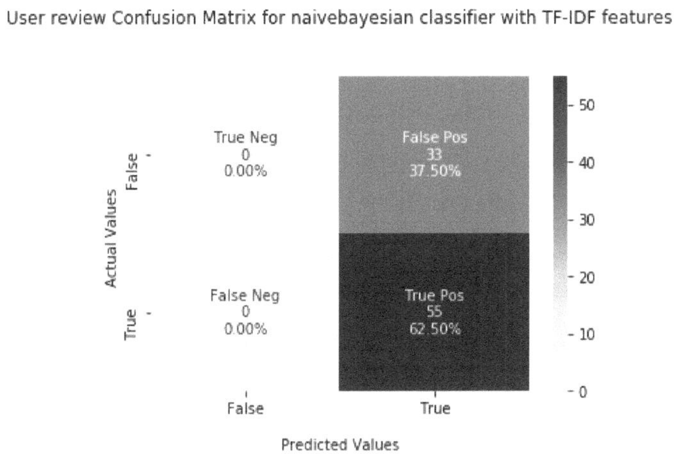

Figure 6.47 Confusion matrix for User review using a naïve Bayesian classifier and TF-IDF

Figure 6.48 depicts the confusion matrix constructed by the RF classifier using TF-IDF as feature selection on the user dataset. The y axis of the created confusion matrix represents the actual values, while the x axis represents the expected values. The GMLSA-recommended method classifies 0 reviews as real negative, 33 as false positive, 0 as fake negative, and 55 as genuine positive. The GMLSA algorithm achieved an overall accuracy of 62.5 percent on this dataset.

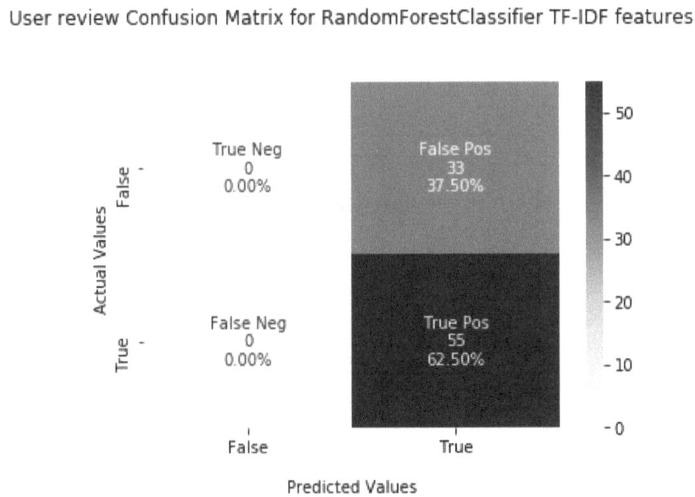

Figure 6.48 Confusion matrix for User review using a Random Forest classifier and TF-IDF

Figure 6.49 depicts the confusion matrix constructed by the LR classifier with TF-IDF as feature selection on the user. The y axis of the created confusion matrix represents the actual values, while the x axis represents the expected values. The GMLSA-recommended method classifies 0 reviews as real negative, 33 as false positive, 0 as fake negative, and 55 as genuine positive. The GMLSA algorithm achieved an overall accuracy of 62.5 percent on this dataset.

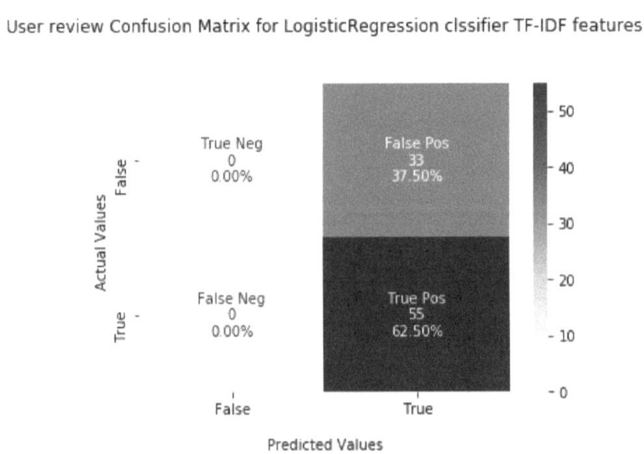

Figure 6.49 Confusion matrix for User review using a Logistic Regression classifier and TF-IDF

Figure 6.50 depicts the confusion matrix constructed by the SVM classifier with TF-IDF as feature selection on the user dataset. The y axis of the created confusion matrix represents the actual values, while the x axis represents the expected values. The GMLSA-recommended method classifies 0 reviews as real negative, 33 as false positive, 0 as fake negative, and 55 as genuine positive. The GMLSA algorithm achieved an overall accuracy of 62.5 percent on this dataset.

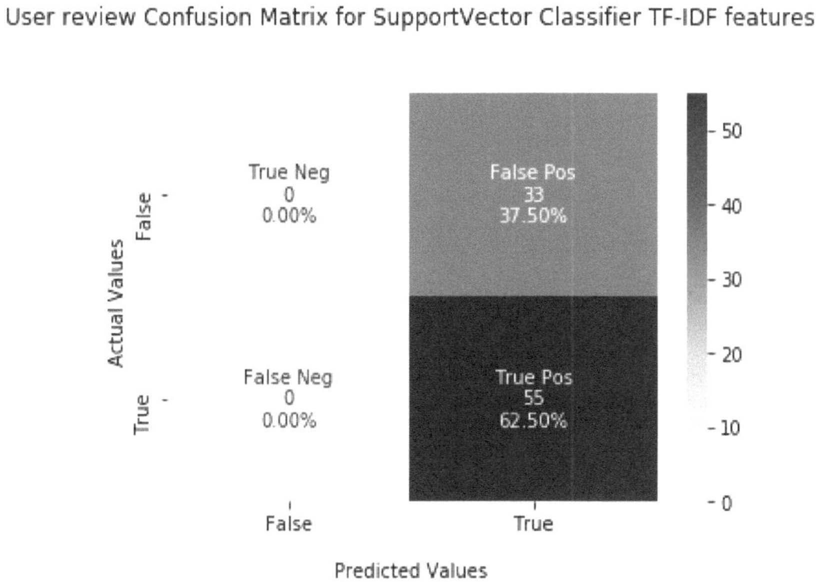

Figure 6.50 Confusion matrix for User review using a Support Vector classifier and TF-IDF

Figure 6.51 depicts the confusion matrix constructed by the KNN classifier using TF-IDF as feature selection on the user dataset. The y axis of the created confusion matrix represents the actual values, while the x axis represents the expected values. Six reviews are classified as real negative, 27 as false positive, 4 as false negative, and 51 as genuine positive using the GMLSA-recommended approach. With this dataset, the GMLSA algorithm achieved an overall accuracy of 64.77 percent.

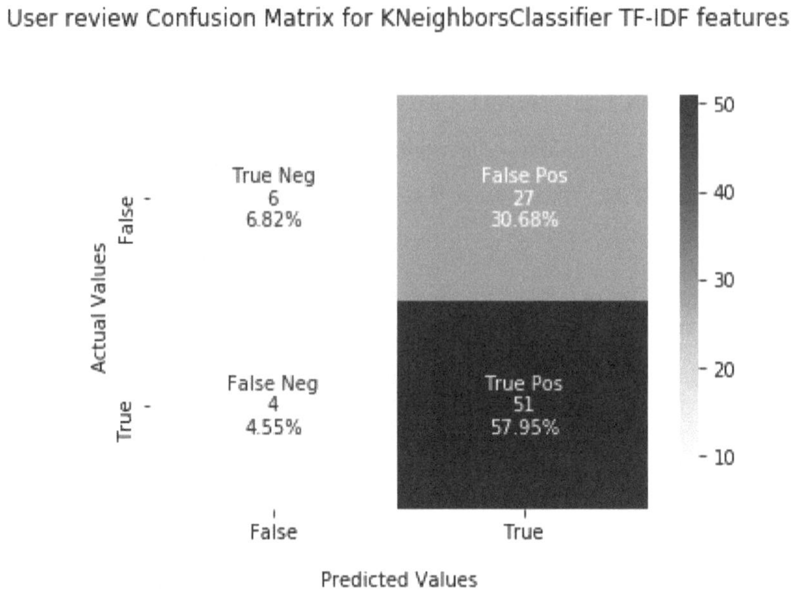

Figure 6.51 Confusion matrix for User review using a K nearest neighbour classifier and TF-IDF

74.19%, 74.19%, 72.58%, 72.58%, and 37.1% accuracy were produced on the user dataset by the NB, RF, LR, SVM, and KNN classifiers, respectively, using the feature selection technique CV.

Figure 6.52 illustrates the confusion matrix generated using NB classifier with CV as feature selection on the User dataset movie reviews acquired manually from the movie viewers review. The y axis of the created confusion matrix represents the actual values, while the x axis represents the expected values. The GMLSA-recommended method classifies 0 reviews as real negative, 16 as false positive, 0 as fake negative, and 46 as genuine positive. With this dataset, the GMLSA algorithm achieved an overall accuracy of 74.19 percent.

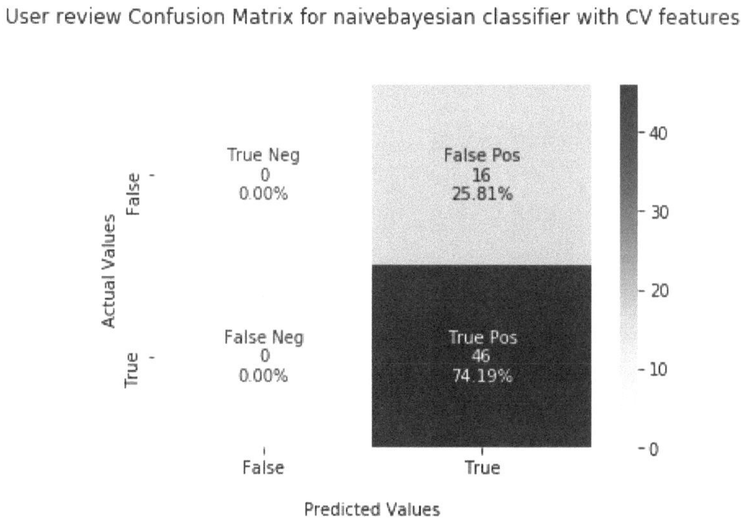

Figure 6.52 Confusion matrix for User review using a naïve Bayesian classifier and CV

Figure 6.53 illustrates the confusion matrix generated using RF classifier with CV as feature selection on the User dataset movie reviews acquired manually from the movie viewers review. The y axis of the created confusion matrix represents the actual values, while the x axis represents the expected values. The GMLSA-recommended method classifies 0 reviews as real negative, 16 as false positive, 0 as fake negative, and 46 as genuine positive. With this dataset, the GMLSA algorithm achieved an overall accuracy of 74.19 percent.

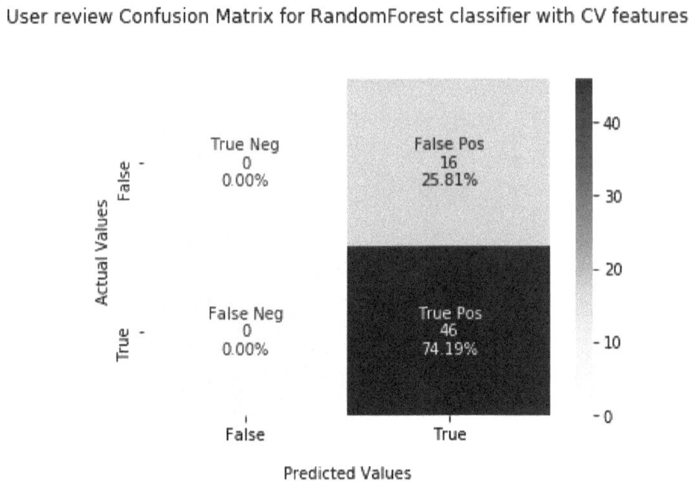

Figure 6.53 Confusion matrix for User review using a Random Forest classifier and CV

Figure 6.54 illustrates the confusion matrix generated using LR classifier with CV as feature selection on the User dataset movie reviews acquired manually from the movie viewers review. The y axis of the created confusion matrix represents the actual values, while the x axis represents the expected values. Using the GMLSA-recommended method, three reviews are classified as true negative, thirteen as false positive, four as fake negative, and forty-two as genuine positive. With this dataset, the GMLSA algorithm achieved an overall accuracy of 72.58 percent.

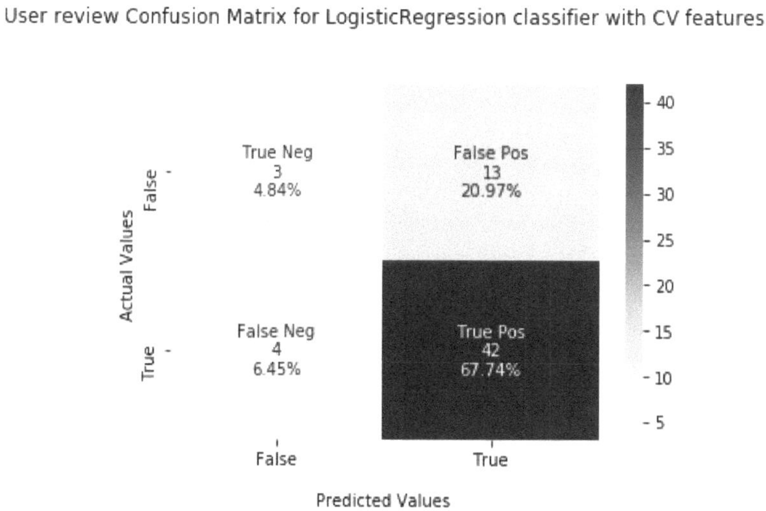

Figure 6.54 Confusion matrix for User review using a Logistic Regression classifier and CV

Figure 6.55 illustrates the confusion matrix generated using SVM classifier with CV as feature selection on the User dataset movie reviews acquired manually from the movie viewers review. The resulting confusion matrix's y axis represents the actual values, while the x axis represents the expected values. Using the GMLSA-recommended approach, 3 reviews are classified as real negative, 13 as false positive, 4 as fake negative, and 42 as genuine positive. The GMLSA algorithm has an overall accuracy of 72.58 percent on this dataset.

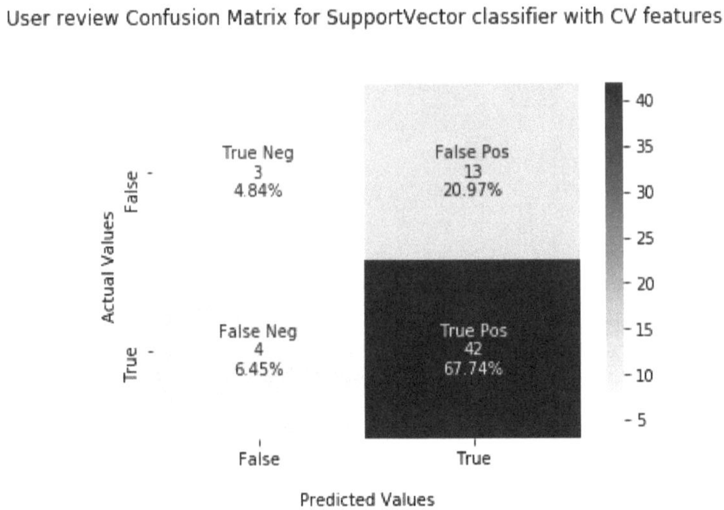

Figure 6.55 Confusion matrix for User review using a Support Vector classifier and CV

Figure 6.56 illustrates the confusion matrix generated using KNN classifier with CV as feature selection on the User dataset movie reviews acquired manually from the movie viewers review. The y axis of the created confusion matrix represents the actual values, while the x axis represents the expected values. 14 reviews are classified as real negative, 2 as false positive, 37 as fake negative, and 9 as genuine positive using the GMLSA-recommended approach. The GMLSA algorithm achieved an overall accuracy of 37.1 percent on this dataset.

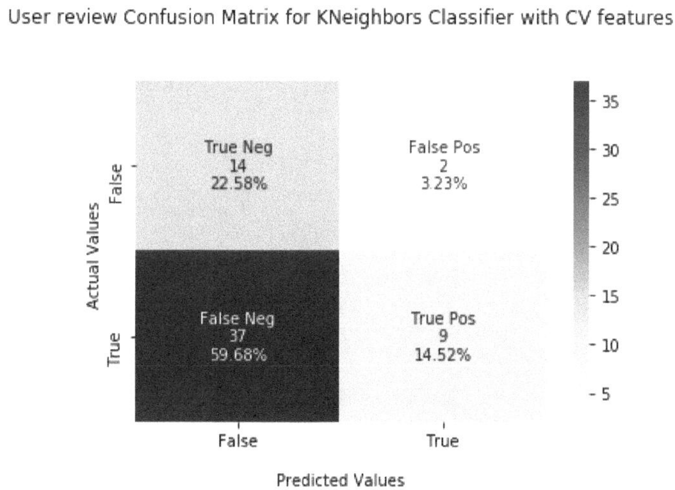

Figure 6.56 Confusion matrix for User review using a K nearest neighbour classifier and CV

Table 6.2 TF-IDF and CV were used to compare the accuracy of all classifiers across datasets.

Dataset Name	Feature Engineering	MNB	RF	LR	SVM	KNN
Gujwebidun iya	TFIDF-Accuracy (%)	88.57	82.86	85.71	88.57	67.14
	CV-Accuracy (%)	89.8	73.47	79.59	81.63	71.43
Hungama	TFIDF-Accuracy (%)	84.83	92.13	95.51	94.38	59.55
	CV-Accuracy (%)	81.6	82.4	84	85.6	66.4
Times of India	TFIDF-Accuracy (%)	94.77	93.6	94.77	94.77	67.44
	CV-Accuracy (%)	91.67	89.17	90	89.17	58.33
User	TFIDF-Accuracy (%)	62.5	62.5	62.5	62.5	64.77
	CV-Accuracy (%)	74.19	74.19	72.58	72.58	37.1
Filmfare	TFIDF-Accuracy (%)	85.71	90.48	85.71	90.48	85.71
	CV-Accuracy (%)	94.83	94.83	94.83	94.83	65.52

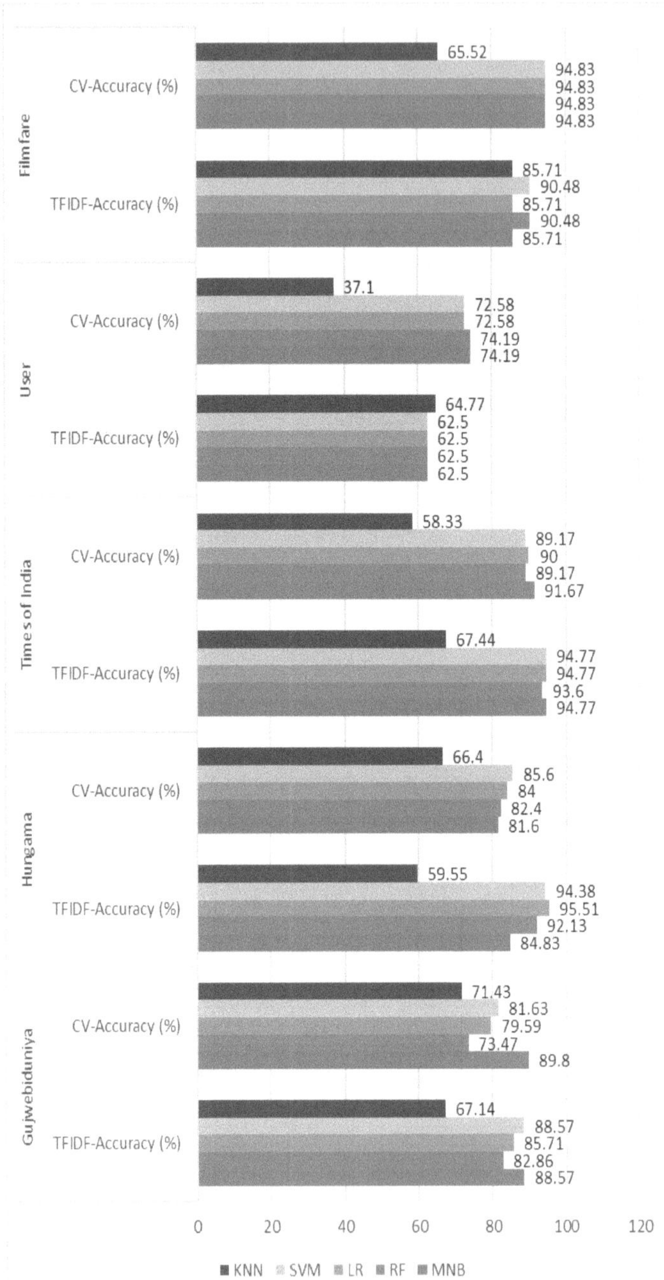

Figure 6.57 TF-IDF and CV were used to compare the accuracy of all classifiers across datasets.

Table 6.3 On the Gujwebiduniya Dataset, all classifiers were compared based on accuracy, precision, recall, and F-scores.

	Model Name	MNB	RF	LR	SVM	KNN
Gujwebiduniya Dataset	TFIDF-Accuracy (%)	88.57	82.86	85.71	88.57	67.14
	CV-Accuracy (%)	89.8	73.47	79.59	81.63	71.43
	TF-IDF-Precision (%)	100	82.86	87.88	88.57	68.75
	CV Precision (%)	100	100	79.59	90	78.79
	TF-IDF Recall (%)	77.14	82.86	82.86	88.57	62.86
	CV Recall (%)	84.85	60.61	79.59	81.82	78.79
	TF-IDF F-Score(%)	87.1	82.86	85.29	88.57	65.67
	CV F-Score (%)	91.8	75.47	79.59	85.71	78.79

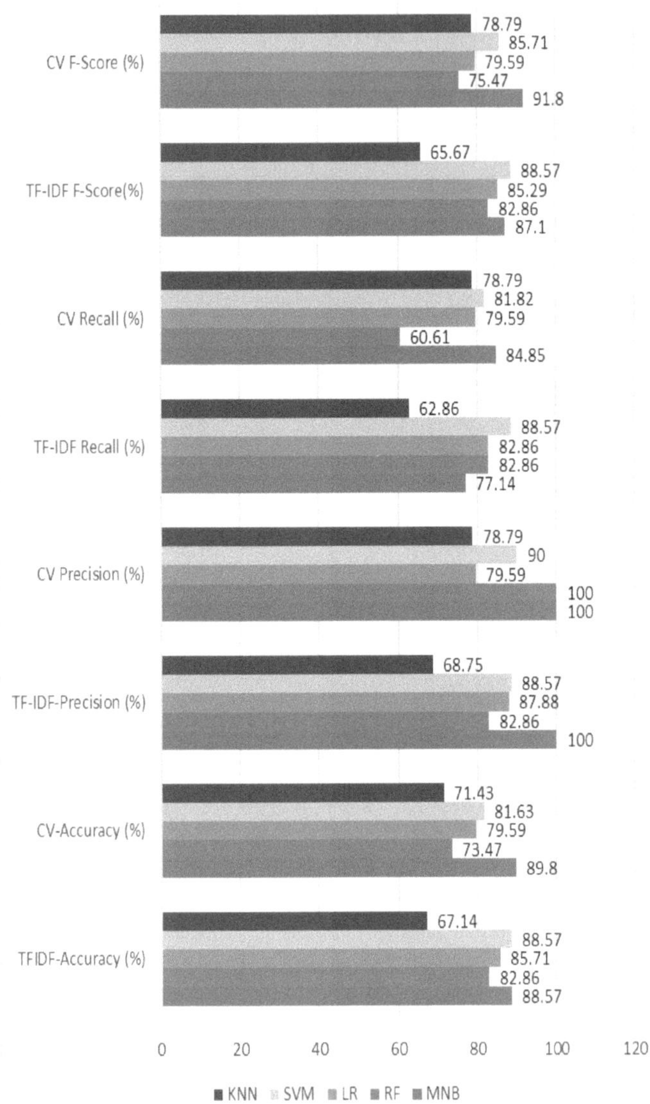

Figure 6.58 On the Gujwebiduniya Dataset, all classifiers were compared based on their accuracy, precision, recall, and F-scores.

Table 6.4 On the Hungama Dataset, all classifiers were compared based on accuracy, precision, recall, and F-scores

	Model Name	MNB	RF	LR	SVM	KNN
Hungama Dataset	TFIDF-Accuracy (%)	84.83	92.13	95.51	94.38	59.55
	CV-Accuracy (%)	81.6	82.4	84	85.6	66.4
	TF-IDF-Precision (%)	77.5	91.58	93.81	93.68	57.05
	CV Precision (%)	74.36	76	84	83.08	78.79
	TF-IDF Recall (%)	100	93.55	97.85	95.7	91.4
	CV Recall (%)	95.08	93.44	84	88.52	42.6
	TF-IDF F-Score(%)	87.32	92.55	95.79	94.68	70.25
	CV F-Score (%)	83.45	83.82	84	85.71	55.32

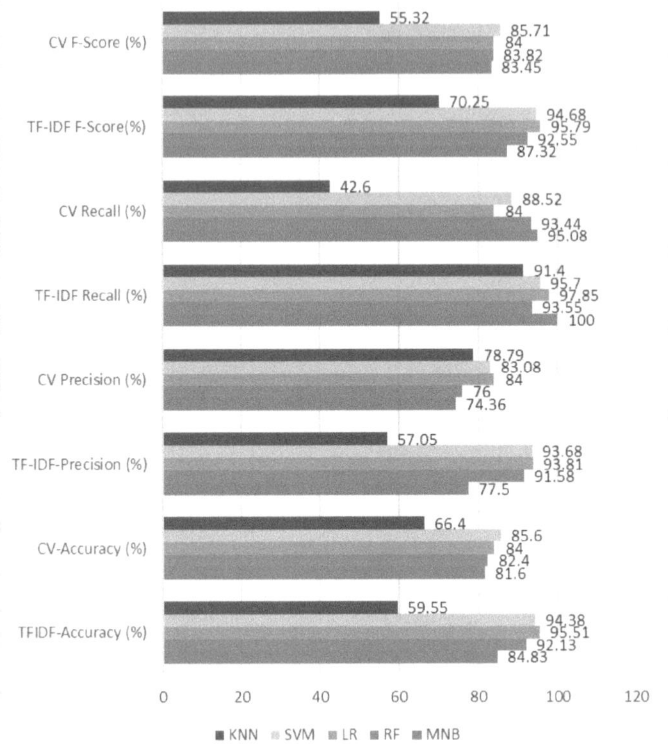

Figure 6.59 . On the Hungama Dataset, all classifiers were compared based on accuracy, precision, recall, and F-scores.

Table 6.5 On the times of India Dataset, all classifiers were compared based on accuracy, precision, recall, and F-scores.

	Model Name	MNB	RF	LR	SVM	KNN
Times of India Dataset	TFIDF-Accuracy (%)	94.77	93.6	94.77	94.77	67.44
	CV-Accuracy (%)	91.67	89.17	90	89.17	58.33
	TF-IDF-Precision (%)	90	91.67	91.86	91.86	59.69
	CV Precision (%)	85.29	86.89	90	86.89	100
	TF-IDF Recall (%)	100	95.06	97.53	97.53	95.06
	CV Recall (%)	100	91.38	90	91.38	13.79

	TF-IDF F-Score(%)	94.74	93.33	94.61	94.61	73.33
	CV F-Score (%)	92.06	89.08	90	89.08	24.24

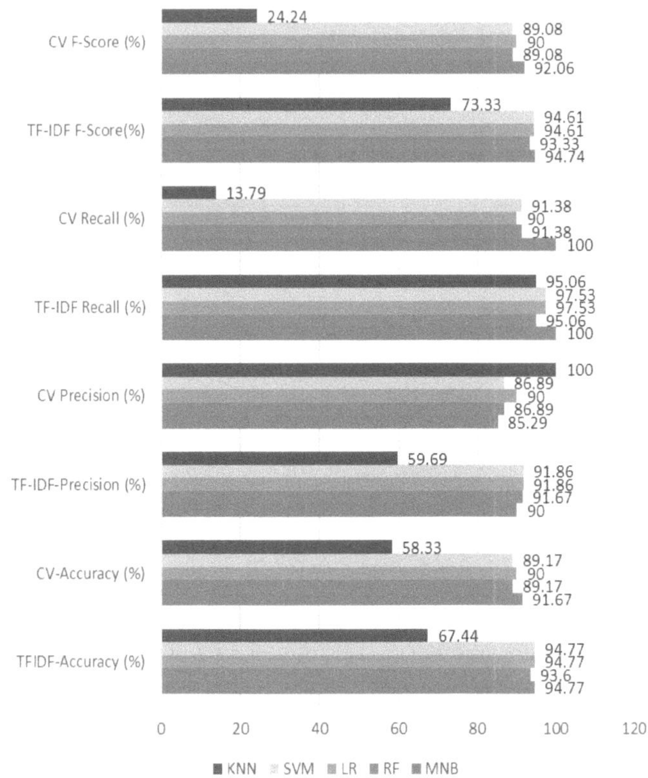

Figure 6.60 On the times of India Dataset, all classifiers were compared based on accuracy, precision, recall, and F-scores.

Table 6.6 On the user dataset, all classifiers were compared based on accuracy, precision, recall, and F-scores.

	Model Name	MNB	RF	LR	SVM	KNN
User Dataset	TFIDF-Accuracy (%)	62.5	62.5	62.5	62.5	64.77
	CV-Accuracy (%)	74.19	74.19	72.58	72.58	37.1

	TF-IDF-Precisio (%)	62.5	62.5	62.5	62.5	65.38
	CV Precisio (%)	74.1	74.1	72.58	78.43	81.82
	TF-IDF Recall ('	100	100	100	100	97.23
	CV Rec (%)	100	100	72.58	86.96	19.57
	TF-IDF Score(%	76.92	76.92	76.92	76.92	76.69
	CV Score (%	85.19	85.19	72.58	82.47	31.58

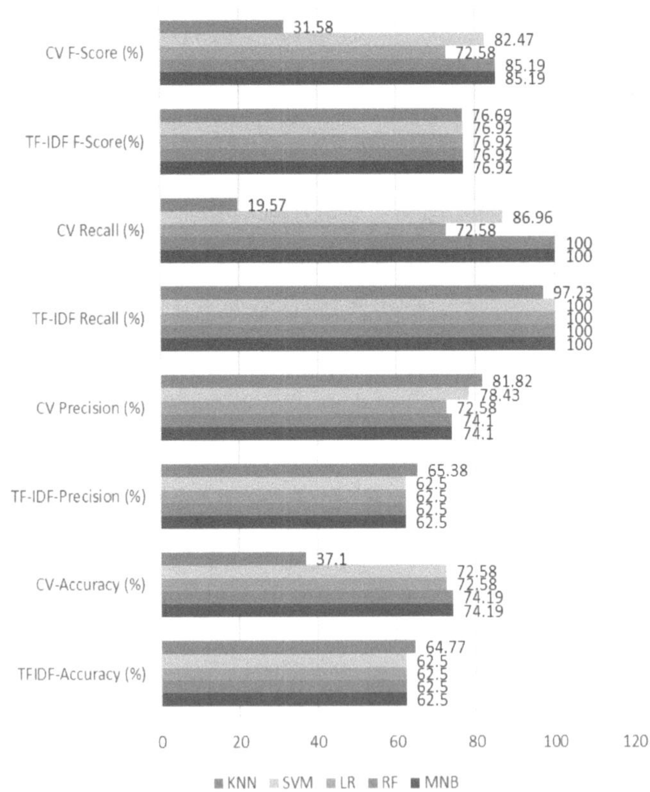

Figure 6.61 On the user dataset, all classifiers were compared based on accuracy, precision, recall, and F-scores.

Table 6.7 On the filmfare dataset, all classifiers were compared based on accuracy, precision, recall, and F-scores.

	Model Name	MNB	RF	LR	SVM	KNN
Filmfare Dataset	TFIDF-Accuracy (%)	85.71	90.4:	85.71	90.4:	85.7
	CV-Accuracy (%)	94.83	94.8:	94.83	94.8:	65.5:
	TF-IDF-Precision (%	85.71	90.4:	85.71	90	85.7
	CV Precision (%)	94.64	94.6	94.64	94.6	90.2
	TF-IDF Recall (%)	100	100	100	100	100
	CV Recal (%)	100	100	100	100	69.8
	TF-IDF F Score(%)	92.31	94.7	92.31	94.7	92.3
	CV F-Score (%)	97.25	97.2:	97.25	97.2:	78.7:

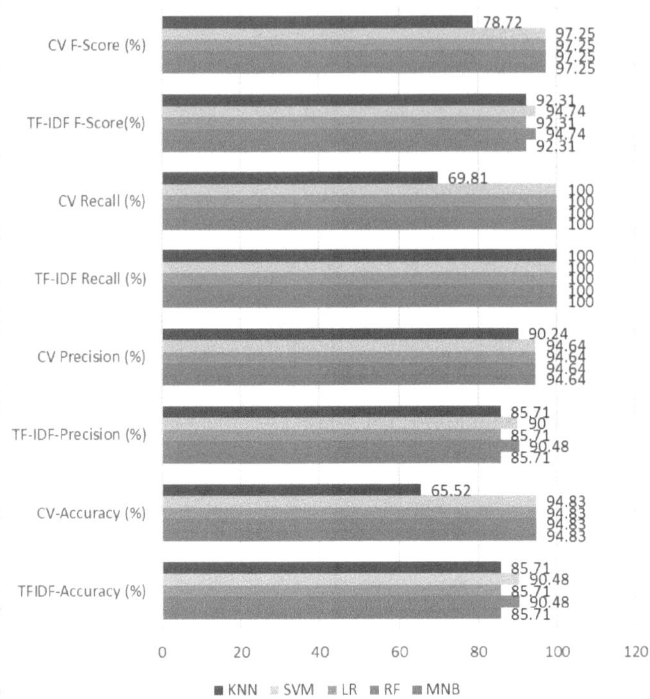

Figure 6.62 Classifiers were evaluated on the filmfare dataset and ranked by their accuracy, precision, recall, and F-scores.

There are five separate Gujarati-language film review databases are tried utilizing two proposed structure designs, results produced are as accessible in table 8. Every one of the five classifier produces higher precision result contrasted with dictionary-based methodology. Considering datasets like Hungama, Times of India and Filmfare, when contrasted with a vocabulary technique, Machine learning methodology has a 10% more prominent precision. ML-based method beats the vocabulary put together methodology by 10% with respect to datasets from Hungama, Times of India, and Filmfare. Datasets like user and Gujwebiduniya, the two methodologies get almost indistinguishable outcomes. Considering the created and differentiated discoveries, not really set in stone that the recommended ML-based system delivers more precise outcomes than the proposed dictionary-based methodology.

Table 6.8 Overall performance-based comparison of ML and Lexicon based method.

Dataset Name	GMLSA						GLSA
	Feature	MNB	RF	LR	SVM	KNN	
Gujwebiduniy Dataset	TFIDF-Accuracy (%)	88.57	82.86	85.71	88.57	67.14	58.18
	CV-Accuracy (%)	89.8	73.47	79.59	81.63	71.43	
	TF-IDF-Precision (%)	100	82.86	87.88	88.57	68.75	56.06
	CV Precisio (%)	100	100	79.59	90	78.79	
	TF-IDF Reca (%)	77.14	82.86	82.86	88.57	62.86	65.48
	CV Recall (%)	84.85	60.61	79.59	81.82	78.79	
	TF-IDF F Score(%)	87.1	82.86	85.29	88.57	65.67	60.4
	CV F-Score (%	91.8	75.47	79.59	85.71	78.79	
Hungama Dataset	Model Name	MNB	RF	LR	SVM	KNN	
	TFIDF-Accuracy (%)	84.83	92.13	95.51	94.38	59.55	63.98
	CV-Accuracy (%)	81.6	82.4	84	85.6	66.4	
	TF-IDF-Precision (%)	77.5	91.58	93.81	93.68	57.05	59.94
	CV Precisio (%)	74.36	76	84	83.08	78.79	
	TF-IDF Reca (%)	100	93.55	97.85	95.7	91.4	77.25
	CV Recall (%)	95.08	93.44	84	88.52	42.6	
	TF-IDF F Score(%)	87.32	92.55	95.79	94.68	70.25	67.5
	CV F-Score (%	83.45	83.82	84	85.71	55.32	
Times of Indi Dataset	Model Name	MNB	RF	LR	SVM	KNN	
	TFIDF-Accuracy (%)	94.77	93.6	94.77	94.77	67.44	63.98
	CV-Accuracy (%)	91.67	89.17	90	89.17	58.33	
	TF-IDF-Precision (%)	90	91.67	91.86	91.86	59.69	59.94

	CV Precisic (%)	85.29	86.89	90	86.89	100	
	TF-IDF Reca (%)	100	95.06	97.53	97.53	95.06	77.25
	CV Recall (%)	100	91.38	90	91.38	13.79	
	TF-IDF] Score(%)	94.74	93.33	94.61	94.61	73.33	67.5
	CV F-Score (%	92.06	89.08	90	89.08	24.24	
User Dataset	Model Name	MNB	RF	LR	SVM	KNN	
	TFIDF-Accuracy (%)	62.5	62.5	62.5	62.5	64.77	53.58
	CV-Accuracy (%)	74.19	74.19	72.58	72.58	37.1	
	TF-IDF-Precision (%)	62.5	62.5	62.5	62.5	65.38	67.25
	CV Precisic (%)	74.1	74.1	72.58	78.43	81.82	
	TF-IDF Reca (%)	100	100	100	100	97.23	58.47
	CV Recall (%)	100	100	72.58	86.96	19.57	
	TF-IDF] Score(%)	76.92	76.92	76.92	76.92	76.69	62.84
	CV F-Score (%	85.19	85.19	72.58	82.47	31.58	
Filmfar Dataset	Model Name	MNB	RF	LR	SVM	KNN	
	TFIDF-Accuracy (%)	85.71	90.48	85.71	90.48	85.71	62.62
	CV-Accuracy (%)	94.83	94.83	94.83	94.83	65.52	
	TF-IDF-Precision (%)	85.71	90.48	85.71	90	85.71	89.14
	CV Precisic (%)	94.64	94.64	94.64	94.64	90.24	
	TF-IDF Reca (%)	100	100	100	100	100	65.71
	CV Recall (%)	100	100	100	100	69.81	
	TF-IDF] Score(%)	92.31	94.74	92.31	94.74	92.31	75.65
	CV F-Score (%	97.25	97.25	97.25	97.25	78.72	

7. CONCLUSION

This study's proposed approach aims to improve the quality of sentiment analysis on textual movie reviews accessible in Gujarati. For doing sentiment analysis on Gujarati text, lexicon and machine learning-based algorithms are proposed. On the lexicon-based side, the authors developed GujSentiWordNet, a sentiment dictionary augmented with a synonym's lexicon, and applied these classification algorithms to five distinct datasets to ensure the accuracy of Gujarati text lexicon-based sentiment analysis (GLSA).On the ML side, author use five classifiers, MNB, SVM, RF, KNN and LR and applied these classification techniques on five different datasets to ensure accurate working Gujarati text machine learning based sentiment analysis (GMLSA). From the generated result of both the proposed methods it is concluded that machine learning based approach gives more accuracy compared to lexicon-based approach. Every one of the five classifier produces higher precision result contrasted with dictionary-based methodology. Considering datasets like Hungama, Times of India and Filmfare, when contrasted with a vocabulary technique, Machine learning methodology has a 10% more prominent precision. ML-based method beats the vocabulary put together methodology by 10% with respect to datasets from Hungama, Times of India, and Filmfare. Datasets like user and Gujwebiduniya, the two methodologies get almost indistinguishable outcomes. Considering the created and differentiated discoveries, not really set in stone that the recommended ML-based system delivers more precise outcomes than the proposed dictionary-based methodology.

8. FUTURE WORK

Sentiment analysis is an analytical approach that determines the emotional meaning of communications using statistics, natural language processing, and machine learning. The ambition of an all-encompassing Digital India cannot be fulfilled unless NLP research and implementation in India is on par with those of languages such as English. Many people find the language barrier to be a significant impediment while using cell phones. As a result, there is an obvious need to expand NLP research for Indian languages so that individuals who don't speak English may go "online" in the proper meaning of the term, ask questions in their native tongue, and get responses.

This path may be made viable by using this study as a basis. Creating industry-specific dictionaries will enable lexicon-based algorithms to be applied to large amounts of data in the future, resulting in more accurate results. In a similar vein, a machine learning-based method may be applied to a large dataset to produce more precise results. Using this study as a foundation in the future may also allow for the implementation of a hybrid technique, which is a combination of lexical research and machine learning strategy.

9. REFERENCES

1. Feldman R. Techniques and applications for sentiment analysis. Commun ACM. 2013 Apr;56(4):82–9.
2. Hussein DMEDM. A survey on sentiment analysis challenges. Journal of King Saud University - Engineering Sciences. 2018 Oct;30(4):330–8.
3. Prabowo R, Thelwall M. Sentiment analysis: A combined approach. Journal of Informetrics. 2009 Apr;3(2):143–57.
4. ZHOU L zhu. Survey on research of sentiment analysis. Journal of Computer Applications. 2009 Mar 11;28(11):2725–8.
5. YANG L, ZHU J, TANG S. Survey of text sentiment analysis. Journal of Computer Applications. 2013 Oct 29;33(6):1574–8.
6. M. V, Vala J, Balani P. A Survey on Sentiment Analysis Algorithms for Opinion Mining. International Journal of Computer Applications. 2016 Jan 15;133(9):7–11.
7. Medhat W, Hassan A, Korashy H. Sentiment analysis algorithms and applications: A survey. Ain Shams Engineering Journal. 2014 Dec;5(4):1093–113.
8. Save A, Shekokar N. A Brief Survey of Sentiment Analysis. In 2020. p. 353–64.
9. Sinha H, Kaur A. A detailed survey and comparative study of sentiment analysis algorithms. In: 2016 2nd International Conference on Communication Control and Intelligent Systems (CCIS). IEEE; 2016. p. 94–8.
10. Rana MRR, Nawaz A, Iqbal J. A survey on sentiment classification algorithms, challenges and applications. Acta Universitatis Sapientiae, Informatica. 2018 Aug 1;10(1):58–72.
11. Chavan S, Puro J, Kawade S, Bide P. Survey of Sentiment Analysis on Social Media. In 2020. p. 441–52.

12. Shah PV, Swaminarayan P. Sentiment Analysis—An Evaluation of the Sentiment of the People: A Survey. In 2021. p. 53–61.
13. Woldemariam Y. Sentiment analysis in a cross-media analysis framework. In: 2016 IEEE International Conference on Big Data Analysis (ICBDA). IEEE; 2016. p. 1–5.
14. Li J, Qiu L. A Sentiment Analysis Method of Short Texts in Microblog. In: 22017 IEEE International Conference on Computational Science and Engineering (CSE) and IEEE International Conference on Embedded and Ubiquitous Computing (EUC). IEEE; 2017. p. 776–9.
15. Jain S, Batra S. Cross Lingual Sentiment Analysis using Modified BRAE. In: Proceedings of the 2015 Conference on Empirical Methods in Natural Language Processing. Stroudsburg, PA, USA: Association for Computational Linguistics; 2015. p. 159–68.
16. Akhtar MS, Kumar A, Ekbal A, Biemann C, Bhattacharyya P. Language-Agnostic Model for Aspect-Based Sentiment Analysis. In: Proceedings of the 13th International Conference on Computational Semantics - Long Papers. Stroudsburg, PA, USA: Association for Computational Linguistics; 2019. p. 154–64.
17. Hu M, Liu B. Mining and summarizing customer reviews. In: Proceedings of the 2004 ACM SIGKDD international conference on Knowledge discovery and data mining - KDD ’04. New York, New York, USA: ACM Press; 2004. p. 168.
18. Wilson T, Wiebe J, Hoffmann P. Recognizing contextual polarity in phrase-level sentiment analysis. In: Proceedings of the conference on Human Language Technology and Empirical Methods in Natural Language Processing - HLT ’05. Morristown, NJ, USA: Association for Computational Linguistics; 2005. p. 347–54.
19. Liu B. Opinion Mining and Sentiment Analysis. In: Web Data Mining. Berlin, Heidelberg: Springer Berlin Heidelberg; 2011. p. 459–526.

20. Kaur J, Saini JR. A Study and Analysis of Opinion Mining Research in Indo-Aryan, Dravidian and Tibeto-Burman Language Families. International Journal of Data Mining and Emerging Technologies. 2014;4(2):53–60.

21. Shah PV, Swaminarayan P. Sentiment Analysis on Gujarati Text: A Survey. Journal of Computational and Theoretical Nanoscience. 2020 Jul 1;17(9):4075–82.

22. Tian H, Gao C, Xiao X, Liu H, He B, Wu H, et al. SKEP: Sentiment Knowledge Enhanced Pre-training for Sentiment Analysis. In: Proceedings of the 58th Annual Meeting of the Association for Computational Linguistics. Stroudsburg, PA, USA: Association for Computational Linguistics; 2020. p. 4067–76.

23. Machová K, Mikula M, Gao X, Mach M. Lexicon-based Sentiment Analysis Using the Particle Swarm Optimization. Electronics (Basel). 2020 Aug 15;9(8):1317.

24. Denecke K. Using SentiWordNet for multilingual sentiment analysis. In: 2008 IEEE 24th International Conference on Data Engineering Workshop. IEEE; 2008. p. 507–12.

25. Kour K, Kour J, Singh P. Lexicon-Based Sentiment Analysis. In 2021. p. 1421–30.

26. Turner Z, Labille K, Gauch S. Lexicon-based sentiment analysis for stock movement prediction. Journal of Construction Materials. 2021 Apr 2;2(3).

27. Sebastiani F, Esuli A. Sentiwordnet: A publicly available lexical resource for opinion mining. InProceedings of the 5th International Conference on Language Resources and Evaluation. 2006 May 22;417–22.

28. Voll K, Taboada M. Not All Words Are Created Equal: Extracting Semantic Orientation as a Function of Adjective Relevance. In: AI 2007: Advances in Artificial Intelligence. Berlin, Heidelberg: Springer Berlin Heidelberg; p. 337–46.

29. Mishra A, Joshi A, Bhattacharyya P. A cognitive study of subjectivity extraction in sentiment annotation. In: Proceedings of the 5th Workshop on Computational Approaches to Subjectivity, Sentiment and Social Media Analysis. Stroudsburg, PA, USA: Association for Computational Linguistics; 2014. p. 142–6.
30. Nielsen FÅ. A new ANEW: Evaluation of a word list for sentiment analysis in microblogs. 2011 Mar 15;
31. Elsaid Moussa M, Hussein Mohamed E, Hassan Haggag M. Opinion mining: a hybrid framework based on lexicon and machine learning approaches. International Journal of Computers and Applications. 2021 Sep 14;43(8):786–94.
32. Azizan A, Jamal NNSA, Abdullah MN, Mohamad M, Khairudin N. Lexicon-Based Sentiment Analysis for Movie Review Tweets. In: 2019 1st International Conference on Artificial Intelligence and Data Sciences (AiDAS). IEEE; 2019. p. 132–6.
33. Hossen MdS, Dev NR. An Improved Lexicon Based Model for Efficient Sentiment Analysis on Movie Review Data. Wireless Personal Communications. 2021 Sep 21;120(1):535–44.
34. Mumtaz D, Ahuja B. Sentiment analysis of movie review data using Senti-lexicon algorithm. In: 2016 2nd International Conference on Applied and Theoretical Computing and Communication Technology (iCATccT). IEEE; 2016. p. 592–7.
35. Bhoir P, Kolte S. Sentiment analysis of movie reviews using lexicon approach. In: 2015 IEEE International Conference on Computational Intelligence and Computing Research (ICCIC). IEEE; 2015. p. 1–6.
36. Jung-Tae Jo, SangHyunChoi. Sentiment Analysis of movie review for predicting movie rating. Management & Information Systems Review. 2015 Sep;34(3):161–77.

37. Mehto A, Indras K. Data mining through sentiment analysis: Lexicon based sentiment analysis model using aspect catalogue. In: 2016 Symposium on Colossal Data Analysis and Networking (CDAN). IEEE; 2016. p. 1–7.
38. Augustyniak L, Kajdanowicz T, Kazienko P, Kulisiewicz M, Tuliglowicz W. An Approach to Sentiment Analysis of Movie Reviews: Lexicon Based vs. Classification. In 2014. p. 168–78.
39. Verma B, Thakur RS, Jaloree S. PREDICTING SENTIMENT FROM MOVIE REVIEWS USING LEXICON BASED MODEL. International Journal of Computer Sciences and Engineering. 2018 Oct 31;6(10):28–34.
40. Yin F, Wang Y, Pan X, Su P. A Word Vector Based Review Vector Method for Sentiment Analysis of Movie Reviews Exploring the Applicability of the Movie Reviews. In: 2018 3rd International Conference on Computational Intelligence and Applications (ICCIA). IEEE; 2018. p. 112–7.
41. PUBLIC SENTIMENT ANALYSIS ON MOVIE REVIEWS. International Journal of Modern Trends in Engineering & Research. 2018 Apr 27;5(4):139–44.
42. Sentiment Lexicon Generation. In: Sentiment Analysis. Cambridge University Press; 2020. p. 227–42.
43. Mehta P, Chandra S. NICFS: A novel feature selection method applied to lexicon based sentiment analysis. Intelligent Decision Technologies. 2019 Apr 1;13(1):41–8.
44. Narayanan V, Arora I, Bhatia A. Fast and Accurate Sentiment Classification Using an Enhanced Naive Bayes Model. In 2013. p. 194–201.
45. Lee S, Choeh JY. Exploring the determinants of and predicting the helpfulness of online user reviews using decision trees. Management Decision. 2017 May 15;55(4):681–700.

46. Rai R, Mewada P. Sentiment Analysis of Movie Review using Machine Learning Approach. IJOSTHE. 2017 Aug 4;5(1):10.

47. Yang Z. Sentiment Analysis of Movie Reviews based on Machine Learning. In: 2020 2nd International Workshop on Artificial Intelligence and Education. New York, NY, USA: ACM; 2020. p. 1–4.

48. Mitra A. Sentiment Analysis Using Machine Learning Approaches (Lexicon based on movie review dataset). Journal of Ubiquitous Computing and Communication Technologies. 2020 Sep 18;2(3):145–52.

49. Rahman A, Hossen MdS. Sentiment Analysis on Movie Review Data Using Machine Learning Approach. In: 2019 International Conference on Bangla Speech and Language Processing (ICBSLP). IEEE; 2019. p. 1–4.

50. Rajpoot V, Agrawal R, Chaturvedi A, Goyal K. An Empirical Study of Sentiment Analysis on Movie Review using Machine Learning based Classification Approach. In: 2021 5th International Conference on Information Systems and Computer Networks (ISCON). IEEE; 2021. p. 1–4.

51. Uma Ramya V, Thirupathi Rao K. Sentiment Analysis of Movie Review using Machine Learning Techniques. International Journal of Engineering & Technology. 2018 Mar 18;7(2.7):676.

52. Mohsin Ahmed H, Rabeea Jaber H. Sentiment Analysis for Movie Reviews Based on Four Machine Learning Techniques. Diyala Journal For Pure Science. 2020 Jan 1;16(1):69–87.

53. M M, Mehla S. Sentiment Analysis of Movie Reviews using Machine Learning Classifiers. International Journal of Computer Applications. 2019 Apr 11;182(50):25–8.

54. Li Y, Wang W, Gao T, Ma J, Deng S. Finding the Key Factors for Movie Influence Using Machine Learning and Sentiment Analysis. In: 2020 2nd International Conference on Machine Learning, Big Data and Business Intelligence (MLBDBI). IEEE; 2020. p. 94–100.

55. Baid P, Gupta A, Chaplot N. Sentiment Analysis of Movie Reviews using Machine Learning Techniques. International Journal of Computer Applications. 2017 Dec 15;179(7):45–9.

56. Parkhe V, Biswas B. Aspect Based Sentiment Analysis of Movie Reviews: Finding the Polarity Directing Aspects. In: 2014 International Conference on Soft Computing and Machine Intelligence. IEEE; 2014. p. 28–32.

57. Kaur G. Text Mining Based Approach to Customer Sentiment Analysis Using Machine Learning. Journal of Advances and Scholarly Researches in Allied Education. 2018 Jul 1;15(6):58–65.

58. Sarkar D, Bali R, Sharma T. Analyzing Movie Reviews Sentiment. In: Practical Machine Learning with Python. Berkeley, CA: Apress; 2018. p. 331–72.

59. Bansal N, Singh A. A review on opinionated sentiment analysis based upon machine learning approach. In: 2016 International Conference on Inventive Computation Technologies (ICICT). IEEE; 2016. p. 1–6.

60. Kaur R. Sentiment Analysis of Movie Reviews: A Study of Machine Learning Algorithms with Various Feature Selection Methods. International Journal of Computer Sciences and Engineering. 2017 Sep;5(9).

61. Pavitha N, Pungliya V, Raut A, Bhonsle R, Purohit A, Patel A, et al. Movie recommendation and sentiment analysis using machine learning. Global Transitions Proceedings. 2022 Jun;3(1):279–84.

62. Singh S, Kaur H. Comparative Sentiment Analysis Through Traditional and Machine Learning-Based Approach. In: Cognitive Behavior and Human Computer Interaction Based on Machine Learning Algorithm. Wiley; 2021. p. 315–38.

63. YETGINLER B, ATACAK İ. Sentiment Analyses on Movie Reviews using Machine Learning-Based Methods. Artificial Intelligence Studies. 2020 Dec 20;3(2):1–12.

64. Jung-Tae Jo, SangHyunChoi. Sentiment Analysis of movie review for predicting movie rating. Management & Information Systems Review. 2015 Sep;34(3):161–77.

65. Tripathy A, Agrawal A, Rath SK. Classification of Sentimental Reviews Using Machine Learning Techniques. Procedia Computer Science. 2015;57:821–9.

66. Sureshkumar G, Zayaraz G. Automatic relation extraction using naïve Bayes classifier for concept relational ontology development. International Journal of Computer Aided Engineering and Technology. 2015;7(4):421.

67. Fouad MM, Gharib TF, Mashat AS. Efficient Twitter Sentiment Analysis System with Feature Selection and Classifier Ensemble. In 2018. p. 516–27.

68. Sharma P, Moh TS. Prediction of Indian election using sentiment analysis on Hindi Twitter. In: 2016 IEEE International Conference on Big Data (Big Data). IEEE; 2016. p. 1966–71.

69. Bhattacharyya P, Chakrabarti D, Sarma VM. Complex predicates in Indian languages and wordnets. Language Resources and Evaluation. 2007 Oct 24;40(3–4):331–55.

70. Bhingardive S, Bhattacharyya P. Word Sense Disambiguation Using IndoWordNet. In: The WordNet in Indian Languages. Singapore: Springer Singapore; 2017. p. 243–60.

71. Bhattacharyya P. IndoWordNet. In: The WordNet in Indian Languages. Singapore: Springer Singapore; 2017. p. 1–18.

72. Garg K, Lobiyal DK. Hindi EmotionNet. ACM Transactions on Asian and Low-Resource Language Information Processing. 2020 Jul 31;19(4):1–35.

73. Mehto A, Indras K. Data mining through sentiment analysis: Lexicon based sentiment analysis model using aspect catalogue. In: 2016 Symposium on Colossal Data Analysis and Networking (CDAN). IEEE; 2016. p. 1–7.

74. Verma G, Verma H. Predicting Bollywood Movies Success Using Machine Learning Technique. In: 2019 Amity International Conference on Artificial Intelligence (AICAI). IEEE; 2019. p. 102–5.

75. Bhagat M. Sentiment Analysis using an ensemble of Feature Selection Algorithms. [San Jose, CA, USA]: San Jose State University; 2018.

76. Karra AK. WordNet Linking. Master of Technology Dissertation, CSE Department, IIT Bombay. 2010 Jun;

77. Bada M, Vasilevsky N, Baumgartner WA, Haendel M, Hunter LE. Gold-standard ontology-based anatomical annotation in the CRAFT Corpus. Database. 2017 Jan 1;2017.

78. Prabhugaonkar NR NAKR. IndoWordNet Application Programming Interfaces.

79. Bada M, Vasilevsky N, Baumgartner WA, Haendel M, Hunter LE. Gold-standard ontology-based anatomical annotation in the CRAFT Corpus. Database. 2017 Jan 1;2017.

80. Panjwani R KDBP pyiwn. A Python based API to access Indian Language WordNets. InProceedings of the 9th Global Wordnet Conference 2018. 2018 Jan;378–833.

81. Morgado da Costa L, Bond F. OMWEdit - The Integrated Open Multilingual Wordnet Editing System. In: Proceedings of ACL-IJCNLP 2015 System Demonstrations. Stroudsburg, PA, USA: Association for Computational Linguistics and The Asian Federation of Natural Language Processing; 2015. p. 73–8.

82. Lakhani S, Jhamb R, Arora M, Kandasamy S. Application of WordNet for Text Analysis in Different Domains. International Journal of Engineering and Advanced Technology. 2020 Jun 30;9(5):774–86.

83. Janani SR, Sathya C, Poornima S. WordNet Sense Disambiguation Based Patent Search. IOSR Journal of Computer Engineering. 2014;16(6):48–52.

84. Hadiya N, Nanavati N. Indic SentiReview: Natural Language Processing based Sentiment Analysis on major Indian Languages. In: 2019 3rd International Conference on Computing Methodologies and Communication (ICCMC). IEEE; 2019. p. 322–7.
85. Sarkar K, Chakraborty S. A Sentiment Analysis System for Indian Language Tweets. In 2015. p. 694–702.
86. Jacob Soman S, Swaminathan P, Anandan R, Kalaivani K. A comparative review of the challenges encountered in sentiment analysis of Indian regional language tweets vs English language tweets. International Journal of Engineering & Technology. 2018 Apr 20;7(2.21):319.
87. Sahu SK, Behera P, Mohapatra DP, Balabantaray RC. Sentiment analysis for Odia language using supervised classifier: an information retrieval in Indian language initiative. CSI Transactions on ICT. 2016 Dec 1;4(2–4):111–5.
88. Singh K. Lexicon Based Sentiment Analysis for Hindi Reviews. International Journal of Advanced Research in Computer and Communication Engineering. 2021 Jan;10(1).
89. Rehman ZU, Bajwa IS. Lexicon-based sentiment analysis for Urdu language. In: 2016 Sixth International Conference on Innovative Computing Technology (INTECH). IEEE; 2016. p. 497–501.
90. Ashna MP, Sunny AK. Lexicon based sentiment analysis system for Malayalam language. In: 2017 International Conference on Computing Methodologies and Communication (ICCMC). IEEE; 2017. p. 777–83.
91. Kulkarni DhanashreeS, Rodd DrSunilF. Word Sense Disambiguation for Lexicon-based Sentiment Analysis in Hindi. Webology. 2022 Jan 20;19(1):592–600.
92. Ali MA, Kulkarni SB. Preprocessing of Text for Emotion Detection and Sentiment Analysis of Hindi Movie Reviews. SSRN Electronic Journal. 2021;

93. Srivastava J, Sanyal S. A Hybrid Approach for Word Alignment in English-Hindi Parallel Corpora with Scarce Resources. In: 2012 International Conference on Asian Language Processing. IEEE; 2012. p. 185–8.
94. Venkataramani E, Gupta D. English-Hindi Automatic Word Alignment with Scarce Resources. In: 2010 International Conference on Asian Language Processing. IEEE; 2010. p. 253–6.
95. Katta E, Arora A. An improved approach to English-Hindi based Cross Language Information Retrieval system. In: 2015 Eighth International Conference on Contemporary Computing (IC3). IEEE; 2015. p. 354–9.
96. Balyan R, Chatterjee N. Factor-based evaluation for English to Hindi MT outputs. Language Resources and Evaluation. 2018 Dec 29;52(4):969–96.
97. Ansari* MZ, Khan L. Techniques for Lexical Semantics in Hindi Language. International Journal of Innovative Technology and Exploring Engineering. 2019 Oct 30;8(12):4075–80.
98. Kawachale SP, Gengaje SR, Chitode JS. Contextual Analysis and Classification of Syllables for Hindi Language. In: National Conference on Signal and Image Processing Applications. IET; 2009. p. 53–53.
99. Soni VK, Selot S. A Comprehensive Study for the Hindi Language to Implement Supervised Text Classification Techniques. In: 2021 6th International Conference on Signal Processing, Computing and Control (ISPCC). IEEE; 2021. p. 539–44.
100. Singh S, Siddiqui TJ. Sense Annotated Hindi Corpus. In: 2016 International Conference on Asian Language Processing (IALP). IEEE; 2016. p. 22–5.
101. Sharma R, Nigam S, Jain R. Polarity Detection of Movie Reviews in Hindi Language. International Journal on Computational Science & Applications. 2014 Aug 31;4(4):49–57.
102. Cernian A, Sgarciu V, Martin B. Sentiment analysis from product reviews using SentiWordNet as lexical resource. In: 2015 7th International

Conference on Electronics, Computers and Artificial Intelligence (ECAI). IEEE; 2015. p. WE-15-WE-18.

103. Mukku SS, Mamidi R. ACTSA: Annotated Corpus for Telugu Sentiment Analysis. In: Proceedings of the First Workshop on Building Linguistically Generalizable NLP Systems. Stroudsburg, PA, USA: Association for Computational Linguistics; 2017. p. 54–8.

104. Naidu R, Bharti SK, Babu KS, Mohapatra RK. Sentiment analysis using Telugu SentiWordNet. In: 2017 International Conference on Wireless Communications, Signal Processing and Networking (WiSPNET). IEEE; 2017. p. 666–70.

105. Gohil L, Patel D. A Sentiment Analysis of Gujarati Text using Gujarati Senti Word Net. International Journal of Innovative Technology and Exploring Engineering. 2019 Jul 10;8(9):2290–2.

106. Se S, Vinayakumar R, Anand Kumar M, Soman KP. AMRITA-CEN@SAIL2015: Sentiment Analysis in Indian Languages. In 2015. p. 703–10.

107. Khurana N. Sentiment Analysis of Regional Languages Written in Roman Script on Social Media. In 2021. p. 113–9.

108. Anagha M, Kumar RR, Sreetha K, Reghu Raj PC. Fuzzy logic based hybrid approach for sentiment analysisl of Malayalam movie reviews. In: 2015 IEEE International Conference on Signal Processing, Informatics, Communication and Energy Systems (SPICES). IEEE; 2015. p. 1–4.

109. Se S, Vinayakumar R, Anand Kumar M, Soman KP. Predicting the Sentimental Reviews in Tamil Movie using Machine Learning Algorithms. Indian Journal of Science and Technology. 2016 Dec 7;9(45).

110. Kumar A, Kohail S, Ekbal A, Biemann C. IIT-TUDA: System for Sentiment Analysis in Indian Languages Using Lexical Acquisition. In 2015. p. 684–93.

111. Jha V, Manjunath N, Shenoy PD, Venugopal KR, Patnaik LM. HOMS: Hindi opinion mining system. In: 2015 IEEE 2nd International Conference on Recent Trends in Information Systems (ReTIS). IEEE; 2015. p. 366–71.
112. Ansari MA, Govilkar S. Sentiment Analysis of Mixed Code for the Transliterated Hindi and Marathi Texts. SSRN Electronic Journal. 2018;
113. Pandey P, Govilkar S. A Framework for Sentiment Analysis in Hindi using HSWN. International Journal of Computer Applications. 2015 Jun 18;119(19):23–6.
114. Pundlik S, Dasare P, Kasbekar P, Gawade A, Gaikwad G, Pundlik P. Multiclass classification and class based sentiment analysis for Hindi language. In: 2016 International Conference on Advances in Computing, Communications and Informatics (ICACCI). IEEE; 2016. p. 512–8.
115. Joshi VC VV. An approach to sentiment analysis on Gujarati tweets. Advances in Computational Sciences and Technology. 2017;10(5):1487–93.
116. Sharma Y, Mangat V, Kaur M. A practical approach to Sentiment Analysis of hindi tweets. In: 2015 1st International Conference on Next Generation Computing Technologies (NGCT). IEEE; 2015. p. 677–80.
117. Das D, Bandyopadhyay S. Building Language Resources for Emotion Analysis in Bengali. In: Technical Challenges and Design Issues in Bangla Language Processing. IGI Global; 2013. p. 346–68.
118. Kumar R, Mansotra V, Kumar T. A first attempt to develop a lexical resource for Dogri language: Dogri WordNet using Hindi WordNet. In: 2014 International Conference on Computing for Sustainable Global Development (INDIACom). IEEE; 2014. p. 575–8.
119. Mohanty G, Kannan A, Mamidi R. Building a SentiWordNet for Odia. In: Proceedings of the 8th Workshop on Computational Approaches to Subjectivity, Sentiment and Social Media Analysis. Stroudsburg, PA, USA: Association for Computational Linguistics; 2017. p. 143–8.

120. Rohini V, Thomas M, Latha CA. Domain based sentiment analysis in regional Language-Kannada using machine learning algorithm. In: 2016 IEEE International Conference on Recent Trends in Electronics, Information & Communication Technology (RTEICT). IEEE; 2016. p. 503–7.
121. Asghar MZ, Sattar A, Khan A, Ali A, Masud Kundi F, Ahmad S. Creating sentiment lexicon for sentiment analysis in Urdu: The case of a resource-poor language. Expert Systems. 2019 Jun 10;36(3):e12397.
122. Medagoda N, Shanmuganathan S, Whalley J. A comparative analysis of opinion mining and sentiment classification in non-english languages. In: 2013 International Conference on Advances in ICT for Emerging Regions (ICTer). IEEE; 2013. p. 144–8.
123. Mittal N, Agarwal B, Chouhan G, Pareek P, Bania N. Discourse Based Sentiment Analysis for Hindi Reviews. In 2013. p. 720–5.
124. Nair DS, Jayan JP, Rajeev RR, Sherly E. SentiMa - Sentiment extraction for Malayalam. In: 2014 International Conference on Advances in Computing, Communications and Informatics (ICACCI). IEEE; 2014. p. 1719–23.
125. Kaur A, Gupta V. N-gram Based Approach for Opinion Mining of Punjabi Text. In 2014. p. 81–8.
126. Prasad SS, Kumar J, Prabhakar DK, Pal S. Sentiment Classification: An Approach for Indian Language Tweets Using Decision Tree. In 2015. p. 656–63.
127. Venugopalan M, Gupta D. Sentiment Classification for Hindi Tweets in a Constrained Environment Augmented Using Tweet Specific Features. In 2015. p. 664–70.
128. Nair DS, Jayan JP, Rajeev R.R, Sherly E. Sentiment Analysis of Malayalam film review using machine learning techniques. In: 2015 International Conference on Advances in Computing, Communications and Informatics (ICACCI). IEEE; 2015. p. 2381–4.

129. Deepamala N., Ramakanth Kumar P. Polarity detection of Kannada documents. In: 2015 IEEE International Advance Computing Conference (IACC). IEEE; 2015. p. 764–7.
130. Ghosal T, Das SK, Bhattacharjee S. Sentiment analysis on (Bengali horoscope) corpus. In: 2015 Annual IEEE India Conference (INDICON). IEEE; 2015. p. 1–6.
131. Miranda DT, Mascarenhas M. KOP: An opinion mining system in Konkani. In: 2016 IEEE International Conference on Recent Trends in Electronics, Information & Communication Technology (RTEICT). IEEE; 2016. p. 702–5.
132. Das D, Bandyopadhyay S. Word to sentence level emotion tagging for Bengali blogs. In: Proceedings of the ACL-IJCNLP 2009 Conference Short Papers on - ACL-IJCNLP '09. Morristown, NJ, USA: Association for Computational Linguistics; 2009. p. 149.
133. Shah P, Swaminarayan P. Lexicon-based sentiment analysis on movie review in the Gujarati language. International Journal of Information Technology, Communications and Convergence. 2021;4(1):63.
134. Shah P, Swaminarayan P, Patel M. Sentiment analysis on film review in Gujarati language using machine learning. International Journal of Electrical and Computer Engineering (IJECE). 2022 Feb 1;12(1):1030.
135. Shah P, Swaminarayan P, Patel M, Patel N. Sentiment Analysis on Movie Reviews in Regional Language Gujarati Using Machine Learning Algorithm. International Journal of Engineering Trends and Technology. 2022 Jan 25;70(1):313–26.
136. Prusa J, Khoshgoftaar TM, Napolitano A. Utilizing Ensemble, Data Sampling and Feature Selection Techniques for Improving Classification Performance on Tweet Sentiment Data. In: 2015 IEEE 14th International Conference on Machine Learning and Applications (ICMLA). IEEE; 2015. p. 535–42.

137. Kumar A. A Survey on Feature Selection Algorithms. International Journal on Recent and Innovation Trends in Computing and Communication. 2015;3(4):1895–9.
138. Fan X, Li X, Du F, Li X, Wei M. Apply word vectors for sentiment analysis of APP reviews. In: 2016 3rd International Conference on Systems and Informatics (ICSAI). IEEE; 2016. p. 1062–6.
139. Spatiotis N, Paraskevas M, Perikos I, Mporas I. Examining the Impact of Feature Selection on Sentiment Analysis for the Greek Language. In 2017. p. 353–61.
140. Ahuja R, Chug A, Kohli S, Gupta S, Ahuja P. The Impact of Features Extraction on the Sentiment Analysis. Procedia Computer Science. 2019;152:341–8.
141. Arief M, Deris MBM. Text Preprocessing Impact for Sentiment Classification in Product Review. In: 2021 Sixth International Conference on Informatics and Computing (ICIC). IEEE; 2021. p. 1–7.
142. Alam S, Yao N. The impact of preprocessing steps on the accuracy of machine learning algorithms in sentiment analysis. Computational and Mathematical Organization Theory. 2019 Sep 16;25(3):319–35.
143. Krouska A, Troussas C, Virvou M. The effect of preprocessing techniques on Twitter sentiment analysis. In: 2016 7th International Conference on Information, Intelligence, Systems & Applications (IISA). IEEE; 2016. p. 1–5.
144. Resyanto F, Sibaroni Y, Romadhony A. Choosing The Most Optimum Text Preprocessing Method for Sentiment Analysis: Case:iPhone Tweets. In: 2019 Fourth International Conference on Informatics and Computing (ICIC). IEEE; 2019. p. 1–5.
145. Duong HT, Nguyen-Thi TA. A review: preprocessing techniques and data augmentation for sentiment analysis. Computational Social Networks. 2021 Dec 6;8(1):1.

146. Pradha S, Halgamuge MN, Tran Quoc Vinh N. Effective Text Data Preprocessing Technique for Sentiment Analysis in Social Media Data. In: 2019 11th International Conference on Knowledge and Systems Engineering (KSE). IEEE; 2019. p. 1–8.
147. Chhajro MA. Multi-text classification of Urdu/Roman using machine learning and natural language preprocessing techniques. Indian Journal of Science and Technology. 2020 May 22;13(19):1890–900.
148. Gupta V, Lehal GS. Preprocessing Phase of Punjabi Language Text Summarization. In 2011. p. 250–3.
149. Kurniawan F BWA. Text Mining Techniques for Identify Islamophobic Conversation Language by Selecting Preprocessing Feature. Research Square Platform LLC. 2021 Dec;7.
150. Pandya SS, Kalani NB. Preprocessing Phase of Text Sequence Generation for Gujarati Language. In: 2021 5th International Conference on Computing Methodologies and Communication (ICCMC). IEEE; 2021. p. 749–52.
151. Gupta V, Lehal GS. Preprocessing Phase of Punjabi Language Text Summarization. In 2011. p. 250–3.
152. Mohan Patro, Ranjan Patra M. A Novel Approach to Compute Confusion Matrix for Classification of n-Class Attributes with Feature Selection. Transactions on Machine Learning and Artificial Intelligence. 2015 Apr 30;

FSC
www.fsc.org
MIX
Papier | Fördert gute Waldnutzung
FSC® C083411

Kolibri 360 GmbH
Ferdinand-Jühlke-Straße 7
99095 Erfurt, Deutschland
produktsicherheit@kolibri360.de

Druck:
CPI Druckdienstleistungen GmbH
im Auftrag der
Kolibri 360 GmbH
Ferdinand-Jühlke-Str. 7
99095 Erfurt